Beyonling

Toward Higher-Level
Thinking and Big Ideas

Patricia M. Cunningham
Wake Forest University

Debra Renner Smith
Literacy Consultant

PEARSON

Boston • New York • San Francisco
Mexico City • Montreal • Toronto • London • Madrid • Munich • Paris
Hong Kong • Singapore • Tokyo • Cape Town • Sydney

Executive Editor: Aurora Martínez Ramos
Series Editorial Assistant: Lynda Giles
Marketing Manager: Danae April
Editorial Production Service: Omegatype Typography, Inc.
Composition Buyer: Linda Cox
Manufacturing Buyer: Linda Morris
Electronic Composition: Omegatype Typography, Inc.
Cover Administrator: Joel Gendron

For related titles and support materials, visit our online catalog at www.ablongman.com.

Between the time website information is gathered and then published, it is not unusual for some sites to have closed. Also, the transcription of URLs can result in typographical errors. The publisher would appreciate notification where these errors occur so that they may be corrected in subsequent editions.

Many of the designations used by manufacturers and sellers to distinguish their products are claimed as trademarks. Where those designations appear in this book, and Allyn and Bacon was aware of a trademark claim, the designations have been printed in initial or all caps.

ISBN-10:   0-205-54217-4
ISBN-13:   978-0-205-54217-8

Library of Congress Cataloging-in-Publication Data

Cunningham, Patricia Marr.
  Beyond retelling : toward higher-level thinking and big ideas /
Patricia M. Cunningham, Debra Renner Smith.
      p. cm.
  Includes bibliographical references and index.
  ISBN-13: 978-0-205-54217-8 (pbk.)
  ISBN-10: 0-205-54217-4 (pbk.)
  1. Thought and thinking—Study and teaching.   I. Smith, Debra Renner.   II. Title.
LB1590.3.C86 2008
370.15'2—dc22

                                                2007009453

Printed in the United States of America

10 9 8 7 6 5 4 3 2 1   RRD-VA   11   10   09   08   07

Photos courtesy of Debra Renner Smith and Jane E. Harriger.

We would like to dedicate this book to our husbands, Jim Cunningham and David Smith, who are willing to accept us when we decide to spend a summer writing about themes and then love us enough to have the perseverance to drag us away from our computers to go on family vacations with our delightful children.

We would also like to acknowledge all the teachers who have welcomed us into their classrooms. We respect your dedication to improving your students' lives on a daily basis. We would especially like to thank Jane "Moe" Harriger, who tried these lessons with her students on a moment's notice, read various drafts of the book, and made numerous helpful suggestions.

contents

Patricia M. Cunningham is a professor of education at Wake Forest University in Winston Salem, North Carolina. She has taught in various elementary grades and has been a curriculum coordinator and director of reading. In 1974, she received her PhD in reading education from the University of Georgia. In 1978, after teaching at Ohio University and serving as director of reading for Alamance County, North Carolina schools, she joined Wake Forest University to direct the elementary education program.

Pat's particular interest has always been in finding alternative ways to teach children for whom learning to read is difficult. *Reading and Writing in Elementary Classrooms,* first published in 1978, is currently in its fourth edition. In 1991, Pat wrote *Phonics They Use: Words for Reading and Writing,* which is currently available in its fourth edition. She and Richard Allington coauthored *Classrooms That Work* and *Schools That Work.* Along with Dorothy Hall, Pat developed the Four Blocks literacy framework, which is currently used as the balanced literacy framework in thousands of classrooms throughout the country. Pat's major professional goal is promoting literacy for all children.

Debra Renner Smith is a reading and writing consultant. She coauthored *Writing Mini-Lessons for Second Grade* with Dorothy Hall and Patricia Cunningham and was a contributing author to *True Stories from Four Blocks Stories,* edited by Cunningham and Hall.

Deb taught kindergarten, second, and fourth grades in Michigan for twelve years and developed curriculum linked to Michigan standards using the Four Blocks literacy model. Deb continues to share literacy techniques at International Reading Association conferences and is currently involved in Four Blocks workshops and staff development that involve training, modeling, coaching, and collaborative conversations with teachers and administrators across the United States. Deb's thorough modeling of techniques provides teachers practical how-to information for immediate success in their classrooms.

Deb excels in discussing best practices when coaching. Her belief is that every teacher can teach reading and writing well and her mission is to help that happen!

acknowledgments

The publisher and authors thank the reviewers of this edition for their helpful comments and suggestions:

- Sheila Bostrom | Thomson Elementary, Brush, Colorado
- Pam B. Cole | Kennesaw State University
- Christine Michelle Eaton | Starside Elementary, DeSoto, Kansas
- Nancy Rice | University of Wisconsin, Milwaukee

Why Higher-Level Thinking?

Higher-level thinking is something that is much talked about but very seldom done. In 1956, Benjamin Bloom published his now famous taxonomy, which classified questions as requiring six levels of thinking: knowledge, comprehension, analysis, synthesis, evaluation, and application. Almost immediately, Bloom's taxonomy became an important part of education theory. We all learned about it in our educational psychology courses. In our methods courses, many of us planned lessons that incorporated the six levels of thinking.

Look back at your educational psychology text (if you can still find it!) or just Google "Bloom's taxonomy," and you will discover that the reason Bloom developed the taxonomy was that he observed that 80 to 90 percent of the questions children are asked are at the knowledge level:

"What was the setting?"
"Who were the main characters?"
"What happened at the end?"

In 1978, Delores Durkin published her landmark study on comprehension instruction. Her observations in reading and social studies classrooms at grades three through six revealed very little comprehension instruction. Moreover, what was labeled *comprehension instruction* by the teachers was actually *comprehension assessment*. Children answered comprehension questions on worksheets and in discussions led by the teachers. Durkin reported that most questions asked during reading and social studies lessons were literal questions that would be classified by Bloom as at the knowledge level. According to Durkin, "The vast majority of the questions focused on facts, many of which were trivial, some of which are no longer 'facts'" (p. 503).

The next level of Bloom's taxonomy is the understanding or comprehension level. Questions at this level ask students to interpret, describe in their own words, or retell. In fact, retelling has become the comprehension goal in most schools. Teachers have children retell a story and compute a retelling score to measure comprehension. Many tests, including the often-mandated DIBELS, use retelling as the only comprehension measure. Using retelling to measure comprehension is better than using a series of literal questions, but it is only one step up from the knowledge level. What about the other four levels? What are we as teachers doing in our daily reading lessons to develop students' abilities to apply? To analyze? To synthesize? To evaluate? Suppose Benjamin Bloom or Delores Durkin was "a fly on the wall" in your classroom and classifying the comprehension discussions you were leading and questions you were asking. What percentage of the time would your students be engaged in applying, analyzing, synthesizing, and evaluating—which together constitute higher-level thinking?

Why Higher-Level Thinking Matters

Why does it matter if most of the thinking we ask children to do as they read is at the knowledge or comprehension level? Why should we worry if our daily instruction does not foster much higher-level thinking? Isn't it enough to teach children to have a basic level of comprehension?

There are many reasons almost everyone is in favor of higher-level thinking and almost no one argues against it. Perhaps the most basic reason for supporting higher-level thinking is that it is the kind of thinking readers do when reading on their own. Imagine that you are on vacation and engrossed in a wonderful book. The book is fiction and, of course, has characters, setting, and plot, which you are keeping up with and attending to but are not what is keeping you engrossed. As you read, your brain is applying the ideas in the story to your own life or the lives of people you have known:

"I am glad I was not born in the eighteenth century. I would never have survived."

You are analyzing what the characters are saying, doing, and feeling and comparing them to other characters—real or fictional:

> "That's just like what happened to my sister when she was traveling in Europe."

You are synthesizing information and making predictions based on this synthesis:

> "I bet she is going to change her ticket and return home just in time!"

Probably the highest-level thinking process we use the most when engrossed in a text is evaluation:

> "It serves him right. He had no right to treat her that way!"

    The first and most important reason for increasing the amount of higher-level thinking we support in our daily instruction is that higher-level thinking *is* the thinking we do as we read. Closely related to and intertwined with that reason is the second reason we should emphasize more higher-level thinking—motivation and engagement. We all want our students to be motivated and engaged in whatever we are teaching them. When children read, we want them to enjoy their reading and appreciate the wonderful world created by the author. Too much focus on facts and summary dampens motivation and engagement. Could comments like these describe your students' reactions to reading?

> "I don't mind reading so much, but I hate answering the questions afterward."
> "Do we have to retell the story again today?"

A steady dose of recall questions and retelling can dampen your students' enthusiasm for books and reading. Higher-level purposes, by contrast, increase motivation for reading because students are reading for the real reasons people read and don't dread the inevitability of the after-reading check.

    Developing students' ability to think critically about what they read is recognized as an important literacy goal in virtually all state curriculum standards and goals. While these goals are stated using different language, meeting all of them requires the higher-level thinking processes of synthesis, analysis, evaluation, and application. In Ohio, students are expected to demonstrate that they can identify and understand an author's purpose for writing. Arizona standards require students to determine an author's position regarding a particular idea and to support it using evidence from the test. Michigan standards require students to analyze themes, truths, and principles within text to create a deeper understanding. Recent data from the National Assessment of Educational Progress (NAEP) confirms our suspicions that while many students have well-developed basic literacy skills, very few students demonstrate proficiency in thoughtful or critical literacy (National Center for Education Statistics, 2004).

One of the best reasons for incorporating more higher-level thinking in your reading lessons is that research supports its role in increasing reading achievement. In 1995, Michael Knapp conducted one of the first research studies to actually observe what happened in classrooms that "beat the odds." Across two years, he and his colleagues observed in 140 moderate- to high-poverty classrooms. Then they compared achievement data and concluded that the teachers with the highest achievement gains did the following:

- Maximized opportunities to read
- Integrated reading and writing with other subjects
- Provided opportunities to discuss what was read
- Emphasized higher-order meaning construction, rather than lower-order skills

In the late 1990s, Barbara Taylor, David Pearson, and other researchers at the Center for the Improvement of Early Reading Achievement (CIERA) investigated classroom practices in schools in which children were beating the odds (Taylor, Pearson, Clark, & Walpole, 2000). Based on their observations and achievement data from seventy first-, second-, and third-grade classrooms, they concluded that the most effective teachers shared these practices:

- Had higher pupil engagement
- Provided more small-group instruction
- Provided more coaching to help children improve in word recognition
- Communicated more with parents
- Had children engage in more independent reading
- Asked more higher-level comprehension questions

Increasing the amount of higher-level thinking students do as they read is supported by our own experiences with what we do as we read, by our understandings of what students find motivating and engaging about reading, and by research that shows teachers who beat the odds put a greater emphasis on higher-level thinking.

The final reason for fostering higher-level thinking is that the mandated end-of-grade tests in virtually all states include measures of higher-level thinking. Some state tests only include multiple-choice questions that ask students to identify themes or lessons learned. Other state tests include questions that require students to write an extended response to the theme of a passage they have read. Perhaps the highest level of thinking is required by the state of Michigan, which requires third-, fourth-, and fifth-graders to construct a written response comparing the themes of two text selections. Consider the kind of thinking it takes for children to respond to questions such as these released items, which are published on the Michigan Department of Education/Michigan Educational Assessment Program (MDE/MEAP) website:

Third Grade
Do you think Eric would want a porcupine as a pet? Explain your answer using specific details from both "Eric's Lizard" and "Porcupine." Be sure to show how the two selections are alike or connected. (p. 10)

Fourth Grade
People can achieve goals when they work together. Do you agree or disagree with this statement? Explain your answer using specific details from both "My Life With Bears" and "Hannah." Be sure to show how the two selections are alike or connected. (p. 8)

Fifth Grade
When you face challenges, you might have to try new things or do things in a different way than people did before. Do you agree or disagree? Explain your answer using specific details from both "Ancient People of the Rock" and "Pioneer Doctor of the Prairie." (p. 10)

Looking at the questions third-, fourth-, and fifth-grade children are expected to respond to makes clear that they are expected to be able to do all of the higher-level thinking processes. They have to be able to apply the selections to their own lives and state their opinions, which requires evaluation. They have to be able to compare two selections, which requires synthesis, and they must support their answer with specific details, which requires analysis. A steady diet of knowledge-level comprehension questions and retelling will not prepare children to do the kinds of thinking required by this and many other state tests.

Why Is There So Little Higher-Level Thinking in Classrooms?

Since reading that emphasizes higher-level thinking feels so intuitively right, is more motivating to students, is supported by research, and is included in some form on most high-stakes tests, why don't we all do more of it? The answer to that question is complex but probably has a lot to do with tradition, with our own sense of uncertainty about how to truly promote higher-level thinking, and with the current obsession with accountability.

First, think about tradition—the way things have always been done. Tradition is the most powerful force in everyone's teaching. When you went to college and enrolled in ed psych and teaching methods courses, you were not a blank slate. You had years and years of experience with teaching—not as the person doing the teaching but as the person being taught. Think back to your experience with reading as an elementary student. Do you remember round-robin reading, in which everyone took a turn and the teacher questioned students randomly to make sure everyone was paying attention? What level of questions do you think your teachers asked? If you could be transported back to your elementary reading classes and could categorize the questions, you would doubtless find the overwhelming majority of them were at the knowledge level.

Surely you remember reading and answering comprehension questions at the end of the selection or in the workbook. What kind of questions do you think predominated during this daily activity? Perhaps you remember meeting in literature circles with your friends as you moved into upper grades. What do you remember about the discussions you had? Literature circles have a greater potential for promoting higher-level thinking, but often the bulk of the discussion focuses on summarizing and retelling the selection.

It is still true that the greatest influence on all of our teaching is how we were taught. All of us have imprinted in our brains hundreds of reading lessons, in which what was called *comprehension* comprised mostly checking on and repeating facts. Certainly, many of us who were studying to become teachers were dismayed by Bloom's and Durkin's observations that the overwhelming majority of questions and discussions were at the knowledge level and vowed to do better. Nonetheless, the tradition in which we learned to read was a powerful force, and most days, we found ourselves teaching as we had been taught.

Now imagine that after your first year of teaching, having figured out some of the management issues and not feeling quite so overwhelmed by the enormity of the task you faced each day in the classroom, you resolved to become the teacher you learned how to be, not the mirror image of all your previous teachers. One of the contradictions you realized as you reflected on what you believed to be best practice and how you were teaching was that most of your reading-related discussions and questions were focused on the lower thinking levels of factual recall and retelling. You wondered what you could do to change that. You realized, of course, that you needed to pose more higher-level questions—but you wondered, What exactly is a good higher-level question? And more importantly in the classroom, What is a good answer to a higher-level question? Obviously, there aren't right or wrong answers that you can easily score, and your retelling scales won't help either!

Most teachers who resolve to ask more higher-level questions discover that coming up with good questions is the easy part. Leading the children to come up with good answers is much harder. Once you have the good questions and the resolve to use them, what should you do next? What should the minute-by-minute instruction look like? Should you lead a discussion with the whole class? Should you put the students in groups and ask them to do the discussion on their own? Because most of us have neither experienced nor observed good higher-level thinking instruction, we don't really know how to do it.

Teaching higher-level thinking requires a lesson framework with some steps and procedures that teachers can lead students through and feel relatively confident that most students actually do the intended thinking. Just posing higher-level questions doesn't ensure
higher-level thinking.

Finally, we have to confront the issue of assessment. One of the reasons for the per-
sistence of factual recall and retelling is that we know how to grade it! This is not just
about putting grades on the report card—although we all have to have some way to justify
those grades. More fundamentally, teachers are concerned with how they will know who is
"getting it." If the questions we pose don't have right or wrong answers, then how will we
know if our students are comprehending? If their response to these questions is all discussion, then how will we evaluate the growth of individual students? Teachers who see the
need for more higher-level thinking and try to promote it in their classrooms often become
discouraged and defeated as they face the realities of accountability and evaluation.

So, what can a smart, hard-working, well-intentioned teacher do to increase the
amount of higher-level thinking when confronted with the obstacles of tradition, uncertainty about the lesson framework, and accountability? The remainder of this book is
devoted to helping you and your students move beyond retelling to higher-level thinking,
beyond low-level facts and details to big ideas. A Thinking Theme lesson framework will
allow you to pose the so-called *big question* and support your students as they think about
the *big idea*. Students will learn to formulate thoughtful answers to the big question, first
orally and then in writing. Finally, they will learn how to evaluate their written responses
and get feedback from you and other students that enables them to revise their writing and
raise the level of their thinking.

The Big Question, the Big Idea, and Deep Thinking

In order to get students to do higher-level thinking—which we call *deep thinking* when talking with our students about it—we need to focus their attention from the very beginning on the *big question*. The big question always relates to a theme—which we explain to our students is the *really big idea*. For instance, we might say, "In order to answer the big question and get to the big idea of the story, we will all need to do some really deep thinking."

Here are some examples of big questions that promote deep thinking about big ideas or themes:

- "Sophie and Wendell [*A Week-End with Wendell,* by Kevin Henkes] have issues getting along all weekend. By the end of the weekend, does Sophie or Wendell figure out how to be a good friend? Why did you choose Sophie or Wendell?"
- "Frog and Toad [*Days with Frog and Toad,* by Arnold Lobel] solve many problems in this book. Did they solve the problems in the same way? Which character do you think was the better problem solver? Why did you choose the character you did?"

- "Is Minna [*The Rag Coat,* by Lauren A. Mills] accepted by the other kids when she finally wears her coat to school? Explain the thinking behind your answer."
- "How did Charlotte [*Charlotte's Web,* by E. B. White] show that she was a good friend to Wilbur?"
- "How do you think Maria [*Too Many Tamales,* by Gary Soto] showed integrity?"
- "Sometimes people cooperate to get something done. How did Grandma and her grand-daughter [*The Wednesday Surprise,* by Eve Bunting] work together to surprise Dad?"
- "Buzzy [*Buzzy the Bumblebee,* by Denise Brennan-Nelson] has one big problem and many small problems to solve. What did Buzzy do that demonstrated he was a good problem solver?"
- "Do Annie and Clover [*The Other Side,* by Jacqueline Woodson] show each other acceptance? Explain your answer."
- "There are lots of characters in *Franklin's New Friend,* by Paulette Bourgeois. Who do you think makes the most effort to show friendship toward Franklin, and how is that friendship shown?"

Sometimes the big question asks children to think about themes across two selections. Here are some big questions that invite cross-text comparisons:

- "Did the characters in *The Great Big Enormous Turnip,* by Alexi Tolstoy, work together better, or did Desmond and Clayton in *The Biggest Pumpkin Ever,* by Steven Knoll?"
- "Compare the characters in *The Wolf's Chicken Stew,* by Keiko Kasza, and *Franklin Helps Out,* by Paulette Bourgeois. They both helped and successfully shared the work so it was easier for everyone. Which character do you think helped the other characters the most?"
- "There are lots of characters in *Stone Soup,* by Marcia Brown, and *Just a Little Bit,* by Ann Tompert. Who do you think showed the most cooperation, and how did he or she demonstrate that cooperation?"
- "Do you agree or disagree that Henry of *Old Henry,* by Joan W. Blos, and Mr. Plumbean in *The Big Orange Splot,* by Daniel Manus Pinkwater, have the freedom to do whatever they want to their homes? How do you know?"
- "Do you agree or disagree that the girls of *Sister Anne's Hands,* by Marybeth Lorbiecki, and Pink of *Pink and Say,* by Patricia Polacco, worked very hard to accomplish their goals? How do you know?"
- "There were many examples of courage in both *Teammates,* by Peter Bolenbock, and *The Butterfly,* by Patricia Polacco. Pick two characters—one from *Teammates* and one from *The Butterfly*—who you think should be awarded a medal of courage. Explain why they deserve the medal."

What Is Theme?

To come up with your big question, look at the selection you are going to have your students read and think about the theme. *Theme* is defined in various ways by different people. Sometimes a theme is defined by a single word or phrase. Courage, friendship, integrity, solving problems, and overcoming hardships are common themes in many children's books. A theme can also be defined as a lesson learned:

"It takes courage to do something you are afraid to do."
"Good friends are there for each other in bad times and good."
"It is better to tell the truth even if you might get in trouble."
"If you don't solve a problem when it is small, it often becomes a big problem."
"You can succeed if you don't give up even when you face obstacles."

Themes are often handed down in a given culture by its proverbs:

"If at first you don't succeed, try, try again."
"The early bird catches the worm."
"Two heads are better than one."

To help children understand theme, we incorporate both the idea of a big concept and a lesson. But rather than make the big idea or lesson abstract, we connect it directly to characters and then help children connect the theme to their own lives.

"Jackie Robinson showed courage when he held in his anger and didn't fight back."
"Charlotte was a good friend to Wilbur because she worked hard to save his life."

Once you have determined the theme—or the big idea of a selection—think about the characters and how they relate to it. Phrase your big question in a way that shows students their opinions—their evaluations—are what you are interested in. Everyone, kids included, likes to express his or her opinion, and phrasing the question in a way that shows kids you value their opinions will engage them immediately and motivate them to do the kind of deep thinking the big question demands.

Thinking Theme Lessons Include Evaluation, Analysis, Synthesis, and Application

The big question will immediately engage your students in the higher-level thinking process of evaluating, but to answer the question, they will also be analyzing and synthesizing. Your students will soon learn that their opinions are valued but must be backed up with evidence from the text. They have to analyze the text to determine what Jackie

Robinson did that showed he had courage. They can't just tell you they think Charlotte was a good friend to Wilbur; they have to be able to tell what she did and how what she did showed she was indeed a good friend.

When you ask children to make text-to-text connections by considering one theme across two selections, you are asking them to synthesize, or put together, what they have learned from two different sources. Jackie Robinson in *The Teammates* and Monique in *The Butterfly* were both courageous people, but they showed their courage in very different ways. As children look at a theme across two texts, they use the thinking process of synthesizing to deepen their concept of that theme.

Throughout the process of helping children think deeply about theme, we are engaging them in the higher-level thinking process of application. We begin the Thinking Theme lesson by asking them to talk with each other about examples and nonexamples of the theme from their own lives:

> "When have you shown courage, and when have you not?"
>
> "Is honesty always the best policy? Is it ever OK to lie?"
>
> "What do you think it means to be a really good friend to someone?"

As students read and analyze stories for themes such as courage, integrity, and friendship, they think about the lessons learned by the characters in these stories and apply those lessons to their own lives.

We call these lessons that help children learn to think deeply about theme and how characters demonstrate that theme *Thinking Theme lessons*. We always begin with a big question that requires students to form and express opinions. To support their opinions, they must analyze characters' actions, thoughts, and motivation. When thinking about the same theme in two different texts, students must synthesize information from two different sources. Throughout a Thinking Theme lesson, we are asking students to apply the theme to their own life experiences. Thinking Theme lessons engage readers in analysis, synthesis, evaluation, and application—all four of Bloom's levels of higher-level thinking.

Choose Stories with Strong Themes for Thinking Theme Lessons

Some commercial reading programs use the term *theme* to include both themes—big ideas authors are telling us something about—and *topics*—dinosaurs, journeys, pioneer life, and so on. Most informational texts do not have a theme. The information is organized around a topic, and the author's purpose is to share information. With the exception of biographies (which are informational texts told in story format), Thinking Theme lessons should be planned with stories that have a strong theme or big idea.

Themes are found in stories, but not all stories have strong themes. The reason we read scary stories is that some of us like being frightened within the safe confines of the covers of a book (and perhaps under the covers on our bed). Mystery lovers enjoy being armchair detectives and following the clues so cleverly planted by great mystery writers. Some stories are written just to make us laugh. To teach children to think deeply about themes, you have to choose stories that have strong themes. When you are considering teaching a Thinking Theme lesson with a story, ask yourself first if the story has a strong theme. If the answer is no, you will be better off structuring your comprehension lesson in a way that leads your students to focus on what the author seemed to intend to do with the story.

Set a purpose for reading a scary story by asking children to decide what was the scariest part and how the author made it scary. When students are reading a mystery, have them list the clues they detect in each chapter and make predictions about what will happen in the following chapter. When students are reading a particularly funny story, ask them to determine the funniest parts and what the author did to make them so funny. Save your Thinking Themes lessons for stories with strong themes, and you and the children will find it easier to answer the big question and justify the answers.

Once you start looking for stories with strong themes, you will find them everywhere. We usually teach our first Thinking Theme lessons using a read-aloud format. Many of your favorite read-aloud stories probably have strong themes, and you can start your Thinking Theme instruction with them. Look at the literature sets used for your grade level, and you will surely find some stories with strong themes. Basal readers always include some stories with strong themes as well. Doing Thinking Theme lessons with the selections from your basal that have strong themes will allow you to teach the adopted materials and promote higher-level thinking at the same time. Thinking Theme lessons are not "just one more thing to do." Incorporating some Thinking Theme lessons into your instructional repertoire will allow you to use whatever materials you have in more engaging and thoughtful reading lessons.

Thinking Theme Lessons Integrate Language Arts and Social Studies

In many states, character education plays an important role in the social studies curriculum. Children learn and think about such important life concepts as integrity, cooperation, and citizenship. Thinking Theme lessons can help children learn and think about these big ideas within the familiar and comfortable confines of a story. By using Thinking Theme lessons, busy teachers can integrate social studies, reading, and writing and accomplish several important goals within a single lesson.

All Students Can Do Higher-Level Thinking

The Thinking Theme lesson framework described in this book was developed for use with students in elementary and middle school and can be used with all kinds of students. The framework was first used in several high-poverty schools in a large city in Michigan, in which almost all the children were African American or Hispanic. Many of the children were English language learners, and more than 95 percent qualified for free or reduced-price lunch.

These schools organized their literacy instruction using the Four Blocks literacy framework, which provides balanced literacy instruction (Cunningham, Hall, & Sigmon, 1999). Debra Renner Smith worked with these high-poverty schools to implement the Four Blocks framework. Across several years, she held workshops, did in-class demonstrations, and coached teachers as they implemented the framework.

As the children participated in this comprehensive literacy framework, increases in their reading levels and motivation to read were apparent almost immediately. Teachers who had taught in these schools for many years realized that they were having more success than they had ever thought possible with their students and redoubled their efforts to provide good balanced instruction every day for every student.

As the framework was implemented, test scores also began to improve. The Michigan reading test, however, is recognized as one of the hardest in the country. As we described in Chapter One, the Michigan test requires students in the third, fourth, and fifth grades to write an extended response comparing theme across two selections:

> When you face challenges, you might have to try new things or do things in a different way than people did before. Do you agree or disagree? Explain your answer using specific details from both "Ancient People of the Rock" and "Pioneer Doctor of the Prairie." (p. 10)

To answer such a question, children must construct a response based on a higher-level, cross-text comparison of theme. Doing so requires high levels of reading, writing, and thinking and is challenging for all students. Doing so was especially challenging for the students in the high-poverty schools Deb worked with.

Working with the teachers, Deb developed the framework for the Thinking Theme lessons that are the subject of this book. The first students to participate in these lessons were all living in poverty, and many were English language learners. In 2005, when the Michigan Educational Assessment Program (MEAP) test was given, more than two-thirds of the students in these schools achieved proficient scores (Cunningham, 2006). Test scores for these Michigan students demonstrate that with a comprehensive literacy framework and explicit instruction, all children can learn to do higher-level thinking and achieve high levels of literacy.

We all know that holding high expectations for all the children we teach is an important factor in determining their success or failure. High expectations alone, however, will not result in higher-levels of achievement or increases in students' ability to do higher-level thinking. High expectations must be combined with daily doses of high-quality instruction that is comprehensive and includes daily instruction in and opportunities for a lot of reading and writing. When Thinking Theme lessons are used as part of a comprehensive literacy framework, our high expectations for higher-level thinking can be met, even with children in high-poverty schools.

A Sample Thinking Theme Lesson

I n this chapter, we would like to take you into a classroom where the teacher is doing a Thinking Theme lesson. We are not going to clutter up this lesson with all the details about how you help children build rich concepts for themes, how you make the Thinking Theme charts, how you organize your classrooms for Thinking Theme instruction, and how you evaluate the progress your children are making with higher-level thinking. Those topics will be covered and many practical suggestions will be offered in later chapters. In this chapter, we just want to give you the "big picture" of what Thinking Theme instruction might look like in your classroom. (If you are a teacher who needs all the details before you can think about the big picture, you might want to skip ahead and read Chapters Four, Five, and Six and then return to this chapter.)

The lesson described in this chapter takes place in the spring. This class has been doing Thinking Theme lessons throughout the year, and the students all know and understand the terms and procedures. The theme for this lesson is problem solving, and the teacher has chosen a delightful text, *Buzzy the Bumblebee,* by Denise Brennan-Nelson.

Upon reading this story, the teacher immediately realized that *Buzzy the Bumblebee* would make a very engaging Thinking Theme lesson. Buzzy has a big problem and must do some clever thinking to solve it. Solving problems is a theme children are familiar with both in books and in their own lives. They will enjoy the story and thinking about how Buzzy will solve his problem. The teacher formulated this big question to focus the children's thinking on the theme of problem solving:

> **Big Question:** Buzzy has one big problem and many small problems to solve. Do you think Buzzy is a good problem solver?

The teacher begins the lesson by displaying the now-familiar theme Concept Chart and writes *Problem Solving* in the center. She asks her students to think about what problem solving means to them. After refusing to see any hands until thirty seconds of "think time" has passed, she gets a variety of responses from the children about solving problems. Together, they come up with a tentative definition of *problem solving*—using your own brain and help from other people to solve a problem or fix something. She reminds the children that they will expand this definition as they think about experiences they have had with solving problems and read a story in which solving problems is the theme, or big idea.

Concept Chart for Problem Solving

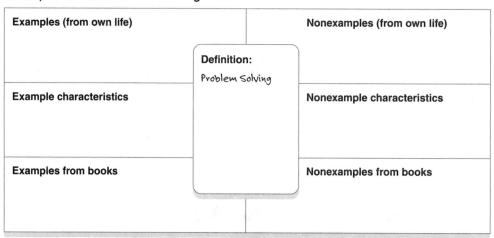

Examples (from own life)	Nonexamples (from own life)
	Definition: Problem Solving
Example characteristics	Nonexample characteristics
Examples from books	Nonexamples from books

Next, the teacher shares with her students three scenarios she has planned to help them think about solving problems.

The teacher has seated the students in pairs to form talking partners. After hearing each scenario, the partners discuss what they think that scenario tells them about solving

Scenario 1

Danny loves to ride his bike, but sometimes the chain falls off in the middle of the day when his parents are at work. The chain is really greasy and messy. Danny doesn't want to break the chain, but he really wants to ride his bike. Should he wait until an adult gets home from work? Should he go ahead and try to fix the chain? Maybe he should just hide his bike in the garage, since his dad said to be careful and he doesn't want to get in trouble!

Scenario 2

Students need school supplies to do schoolwork. Teachers do not like to hear excuses, but sometimes students leave their book bags at home. Maya has forgotten her book bag. What should she do? She does not want to lose recess for not being prepared for school. She could ask her friends for a pencil and paper, but maybe they will tell on her. How might she solve her problem?

Scenario 3

Most children love recess. They get to play basketball, jump rope, and play soccer. Sometimes when the bell rings, the children run to line up and forget to bring in a jump rope or ball. What if the basketballs, jump ropes, and soccer balls all disappeared one day? Then what would the children do outside? Not putting things away is a problem. Does the teacher need to solve the problem, or can the children solve it on their own? What rules should there be?

problems. Volunteers then share what the partners discussed. The teacher reminds the students that we all have problems, and the sooner we try to solve them, the better. Sometimes little problems become big problems if we ignore them and don't try to solve them.

Next the teacher puts the children into groups of three or four, and they discuss their own experiences with solving problems. The teacher asks the groups to try to come up with examples of clever problem solving as well as examples in which the problem was not solved and became a bigger problem (nonexamples). Here's the discussion of one small group:

Chelsea: My mom is always pestering me to put my stuff away so people won't steal it.

Jamal: My parents do that too!

Chelsea: Well, one time I was so tired after softball practice that I left my bike on the sidewalk by the garage. My dad even reminded me to put away my bike. But I didn't do it.

Jamal: Oh, no!

Maria: What happened to your bike?

Chelsea: I thought it was stolen because in the morning it was gone. [Jamal and Maria gasp.] My dad hid it in the basement and didn't tell me for a whole week! I solved my problem by never leaving my bike out ever again.

Jamal and Maria told stories about their experiences with solving problems. Jamal's skateboard was stolen when he left it out. Maria had no place to put her bike inside, but she bought a padlock for it at a yard sale and that solved the problem!

After six minutes of small-group discussion, the class gathers together and shares their own experiences. Then they add characteristics and examples to the Concept Chart for Problem Solving.

Concept Chart for Problem Solving

Examples (from own life)		Nonexamples (from own life)
Put things away or locked them up Helped my sister fix broken toy Talked about friend's hurt feelings and apologized to her	**Definition:** Problem Solving— using your own brain and help from other people to solve a problem or fix something	Didn't listen to my dad Ignored someone who fell down Would not give the little boy a bandage Teased the other girls in the classroom
Example characteristics Helping other people with stuff Fixing things that break Talking about a problem with the person causing it Figuring out what is wrong and fixing it		**Nonexample characteristics** Ignoring the problem Arguing, disagreeing Walking away instead of helping
Examples from books		**Nonexamples from books**

Next the teacher focuses the children's attention on the Thinking Theme Chart. The big question is provided at the top of the chart, and the children review the familiar columns they will fill in as they discuss events related to the theme. They read the big question together and review what goes in each column. The first column is where they will list the events and actions they think relate to the theme. In the next column, they will record why they think that event happened. In the third column, they will list what the character got out of doing that action. Finally, they will try to decide if the event is a good example of the theme—problem solving.

Thinking Theme Chart for Problem Solving

Big Question:			
Buzzy has one big problem and many small problems to solve. Do you think Buzzy is a good problem solver?			
Event or **actions** by characters connected to the theme, including examples and nonexamples	**Why** does the character act this way?	What does the character **get** for acting this way?	Does this event show the **theme** of problem solving? Yes, because *or* No, because

Next the teacher introduces *Buzzy the Bumblebee,* written by Denise Brennan-Nelson. A story summary is included to help you, the teacher, understand what is happening in the lesson. (We do not share summaries with our students before they read. Doing so would ruin the suspense of the story.)

Summary of *Buzzy the Bumblebee*

Buzzy is a bumblebee who, like all bumblebees, loves to fly. Buzzy is unusual, however, in that he also loves to read! One day, he reads that "Bumblebees weren't meant to fly." He gets so worried about this that he loses his confidence, and when he tries to fly, his wings just won't work. Buzzy is very unhappy, because he has always loved flying. Also, not being able to fly creates many problems to solve. How will he get home if he can't fly? Eventually, by climbing and floating and walking (actions he has never before done!), Buzzy gets home. Reassured by his parents that if he believes in himself, he will indeed be able to fly, Buzzy once again takes flight.

The teacher tells students that before they can begin reading about Buzzy and figure out what his problem is and how he solves it, they need to think about some important vocabulary that will help them understand the story. She has students look at some of the pictures and shows how the pictures can help them build meanings for words. The teacher has written these seven words on index cards:

She teaches this vocabulary by using pictures and words from the story. Because she doesn't want to give away how the story ends, she passes by many pages without letting the children see them and only uses pages from the first half of the story. On page 2, she uses the pictures to introduce *Buzzy* and *bumblebee*. The children identify them in the picture and pronounce the words *Buzzy* and *bumblebee* on the index cards. She quickly turns to page 10 and shows the children the word *stranded* on the index card. They pronounce the word *stranded* with her, and she reads a sentence to them that indicates that Buzzy was stranded on a flower and wanted to fly away. The children quickly understand that the word *stranded* means "stuck there." Since they haven't read the story yet, they wonder why he just doesn't fly away. "Is he hurt?" they ask. The teacher tells them that they will soon find out why he doesn't fly away and that not being able to fly is a big part of his problem.

Quickly turning to page 14, the teacher shows students the word *dragonflies*. They pronounce *dragonflies* with her and find the dragonflies in the picture. Before turning to page 16, the teacher has students pronounce the final three words she has written on index cards: *stream, frustration,* and *destination*. They identify the stream in the picture on page 16. Then they use the context and their own experiences to determine what *frustration* means, and they know that the *destination* is the place Buzzy is trying to get to. They now know that he can't fly, but they don't know why. This teacher has very cleverly used the story sparingly to introduce vocabulary and pique their curiosity!

The children are very eager to get their hands on the books after this titillating vocabulary introduction. Before giving them the books, however, the teacher points out the sticky flags she has placed at the bottom of pages 7, 13, and 15 in each book. She reminds the students that she has placed the sticky flags at points where she wants them to stop and think about the events and other information they will fill in after reading on the Thinking Theme Chart.

> "Today, you have three sticky flags. Stop at each one, and talk with your partner about what has happened so far in the story and what it tells you about Buzzy and problem solving. The sticky flag on page 16 also reminds you that that is our stopping point for today. We will read and think about the rest of the story tomorrow."

Stop and think!

The students understand that the sticky flag allows them to chunk the selection in pieces and builds in time for them to reflect and discuss. The teacher tells the students that they will be reading with their reading partners today and that she will be coming around to coach them as they read.

"What is your job as you are reading today?" she asks before handing each set of partners one book. The children quickly respond that their job is to find events that tell something about the characters and the theme of problem solving and that they should be ready to share those events so they can be listed on the Thinking Theme Chart. The teacher sets the timer for fourteen minutes, reminding the children that if they finish reading and talking about the story and there is still time, they should write down one event they want to add to the chart and what they think should go in the *Why, Get,* and *Theme* columns.

The children quickly get with their partners and take their books to quiet spots to read. They begin reading and it's clear from the way they look at the Concept Chart for Problem Solving and the Thinking Theme Chart that they are thinking about the things the characters do and what that tells them about the theme. The teacher circulates, spending a few minutes with four or five partnerships and coaching them in their reading and thinking.

After fourteen minutes, the timer sounds and the children gather together to share their thinking and complete the chart based on the first half of the story. The teacher leads them in listing events that happened in the story that tell something about problem solving. As each event is listed, the teacher leads students through the Thinking Theme steps by working across the columns.

After listing *Buzzy climbs down from the flower,* the teacher asks,

> "Now we have an event that we think tells us something about problem solving, what is our next step?"

A Sample Thinking Theme Lesson

After the students respond "*Why,*" the teacher expands this answer to include the whole key question:

"**Why** did the character act that way? Why did Buzzy climb down?"

She listens to several explanations of why he climbs down and then captures the group's thinking by writing

He has to get down and he thinks he can't fly.

Pointing to the third column, the teacher asks,

"What is our next key word?"

The students answer, "*Get.*" The teacher acknowledges their correct response and expands their answer:

"Yes exactly! What did the character *get* for acting this way?"

Again, the teacher listens to several responses and then summarizes their thinking:

"He gets down, but he almost slipped and fell."

The teacher then asks the students to verbalize the next step in the Thinking Theme process:

"What is the key word for the last column?"

The students chime in unison "*Theme.*" The teacher expands their answer again:

"Yes, the next step is deciding what the event tells us about the theme."

One student responds, "Yes, because he doesn't stay up there the rest of his life." Everyone laughs and the teacher records these exact words, because they comprise a right-on-target answer to this question.

Today's lesson ends as one more event is listed and the children come up with answers for the **Why, Get,** and **Theme** columns. The teacher congratulates the children on the good partner cooperation she saw all of them exhibit and tells them they will finish the story and see if Buzzy does indeed get home tomorrow. It is clear that the children are eager to see how the story turns out.

Thinking Theme Chart for Problem Solving: continued

Big Question:			
Buzzy has one big problem and many small problems to solve. Do you think Buzzy is a good problem solver?			
Event or **actions** by characters connected to the theme, including examples and nonexamples	**Why** does the character act this way?	What does the character **get** for acting this way?	Does this event show the **theme** of problem solving? Yes, because or No, because
Buzzy reads that bees can't fly.	He likes to read and usually believes what he reads.	He is confused and unhappy. He used to fly, but now he is convinced that he can't.	This is the start of the problem Buzzy has to solve.
Buzzy climbs down from the flower.	He has to get down, and he thinks he can't fly.	He gets down, but he almost slips and falls.	Yes, because he doesn't stay up there the rest of his life.
Buzzy asks the dragonflies to walk with him.	He is scared and lonely.	He is envious and mad that the dragonflies won't walk with him.	Yes, because he is trying to get help to solve his problems.

On the following day, the teacher and children review the concept of problem solving using the information included on the Concept Chart for Problem Solving. They also review the information they have listed on the Thinking Theme Chart. The teacher tells the students that they will be reading in teams today. She appoints a coach in each group and makes sure group members know that their coach will stop them when they get to the sticky flags.

Stop and think!

> "When you get to each sticky flag, I want your group to decide on one event you want to add to our chart from that portion of the text."

The teacher appoints a recorder in each group and tells members that their recorder will write down the one event they choose. When the groups have finished reading and have several events written down, the teacher asks them to spend the rest of their time talking about what they think should go in the **Why, Get,** and **Theme** columns. She sets the timer for eighteen minutes, and the children quickly assemble in their groups and begin to read. She circulates among the groups, reminding them of their task and coaching them on their thinking. She also supports the coach and recorder in each group, reminding the children of the behaviors she expects when they are reading together in teams.

When the timer sounds, the class quickly reassembles. The groups are all eager to share the events they have written down, and they are ready with answers for the **Why, Get,** and **Theme** columns.

Thinking Theme Chart for Problem Solving: Completed

Big Question:			
Buzzy has one big problem and many small problems to solve. Do you think Buzzy is a good problem solver?			
Event or **actions** by characters connected to the theme, including examples and nonexamples	**Why** does the character act this way?	What does the character **get** for acting this way?	Does this event show the **theme** of problem solving? Yes, because or No, because
Buzzy reads that bees can't fly.	He likes to read and usually believes what he reads.	He is confused and unhappy. He used to fly, but now he is convinced that he can't.	This is the start of the problem Buzzy has to solve.
Buzzy climbs down from the flower.	He has to get down, and he thinks he can't fly.	He gets down, but he almost slips and falls.	Yes, because he doesn't stay up there the rest of his life.
Buzzy asks the dragonflies to walk with him.	He is scared and lonely.	He is envious and mad that the dragonflies won't walk with him.	Yes, because he is trying to get help to solve his problems.
Buzzy trudges through the grass, trying to get home to his family.	He doesn't think he can fly, and he has to get home.	He is tired and worried he will never be able to fly again.	Yes, he needs to get home so walking works.
Buzzy makes a boat from a feather and floats home.	He has to cross the stream and he can't swim.	He is joyful and relieved.	Yes, he is still heading home.
Buzzy runs the rest of the way home through the tall grass.	He is afraid, alone, and worried.	He is tired.	Yes, he is still heading home.
Buzzy realizes he can fly after talking to his parents.	His parents tell him to believe in himself.	He has the confidence to fly. He is proud that he solved the problem of how to get home. He realizes he shouldn't believe everything he reads; he should use common sense, too.	Yes, he solved his problem because now he can fly again.

After completing the Thinking Theme Chart, the teacher and children add several examples of good problem solving to the Concept Chart for Problem Solving. They also decide that Buzzy's believing bumblebees can't fly from reading the book is not good problem solving and should be listed as a nonexample. Here is what the Concept Chart on solving problems looked like with examples and nonexamples from this selection added.

Concept Chart for Problem Solving: Completed

Examples (from own life)	Nonexamples (from own life)

Put things away or locked them up
Helped my sister fix broken toy
Talked about friend's hurt
  feelings and apologized to her
	Didn't listen to my dad
	Ignored someone who fell down
	  Would not give the little boy a
	  bandage
	Teased the other girls in the
	  classroom

Definition:

Problem Solving—using your own brain and help from other people to solve a problem or fix something

Example characteristics	Nonexample characteristics

Helping other people with stuff
Fixing things that break
Talking about a problem with
  the person causing it
Figuring out what is wrong
  and fixing it
	Ignoring the problem
	Arguing, disagreeing
	Walking away instead of helping

Examples from books	Nonexamples from books
Buzzy figures out how to climb down from the plant, even though he has never done it before. Buzzy makes a boat from a feather to float across the stream. Buzzy realizes he couldn't fly because he lost confidence in his ability to fly.	Buzzy does not fly home after reading the book because he believes the book and not in himself and his ability to fly.

When they have completed the chart, the teacher tells the students they have done their jobs very well and have done excellent thinking about solving problems. She then writes a prompt on the board:

Buzzy has one big problem and many small problems to solve. Do you think Buzzy is a good problem solver? State your opinion clearly, and back up your opinion with specific details and examples from this story.

The children quickly take out their reading-response notebooks and begin to write. Clearly, they have all done this type of writing about characters and themes before and are comfortable and confident in expressing their opinions and backing them up. As the children write, it is obvious they are using the Concept Chart and the Thinking Theme Chart to construct their responses. As the children write, the teacher circulates, stopping to coach children who need some extra support to complete this complex task.

When the writing time is up, the teacher gathers the students and volunteers read what they have written. Not everyone chose the same events to explain how Buzzy solves his problems, but everyone has good reasons for his or her choices. After each child shares, the teacher points to the Thinking Theme Checklist for a single text displayed on the wall.

Thinking Theme Checklist for a Single Text

❏   1. Do I take a position and clearly answer the question?

❏   2. Do I include my definition of the theme?

❏   3. Do I support my answer with specific examples and details from the selection?

❏   4. Is my response complete?

The teacher points out that each student who read did all four things on the Thinking Theme Checklist. Each took a position on Buzzy's problem-solving ability, each defined the theme in his or her own words, each supported that position with specific examples and details from the story, each gave a complete response.

After several children have had a chance to share, the teacher asks all the students to look at their own writing and give themselves checks for the four items on the checklists. She tells them,

> "If you can't give your writing a check for any of the four items or if you are not sure, raise your hand and I will come and help you fix it."

The lesson ends with the children reading their own responses to make sure they have clearly stated a position, supported it with specific examples and details from the text, and written a complete response. The teacher helps several children add to their response so they can give themselves all four checks.

We hope this example of a Thinking Theme lesson has given you a good sense of what the process looks like once the teacher and class are comfortable with the Thinking Theme lesson framework. In the next three chapters of the book, we will describe the specific procedures used to develop the Concept Chart, complete the Thinking Theme Chart, and teach children how to write and evaluate a Thinking Theme response.

Teaching a Thinking Theme Lesson for a Single Text

1. Choose a story with a strong theme that includes several events that are examples and nonexamples of the theme.
2. Place sticky flags in the text at the bottom of pages on which theme-related events occur.
3. Come up with a big question that connects the characters with the theme.
4. Present three theme-related scenarios to students.
5. Form students into small groups, and have their share their personal experiences with the theme.
6. With your students, create a Concept Chart for the theme based on the scenarios and students' personal experiences with the theme.
7. Introduce the story to the class along with the big question they will need to do deep thinking about.
8. Introduce the characters' names and other key vocabulary.
9. Show children the Thinking Theme Chart they will complete after reading, and review what goes in each column.
10. Have children read all or part of the story, stopping at the sticky flags to reflect on the characters' actions and the theme.
11. Complete the Thinking Theme Chart together.
12. Complete the Concept Chart by adding examples and nonexamples from the story.
13. Have children write their answers to the big question, backing up their opinions with facts and details from the story.
14. Have children evaluate their responses using the Thinking Theme Checklist.

Making the Concept of Theme Kid Friendly

I n order to think deeply about a theme, children need to have a rich concept of what that theme means. Children cannot really consider how courageous a character is or which character shows the most integrity if they have a limited definitional knowledge of the key concept. It is not enough to know that *courage* is another word for *bravery* or that *integrity* means "telling the truth." Children need to have a rich knowledge of what these concepts mean if they are going to think deeply about them.

To build theme concepts, we use an adaptation of the *Frayer model* of concept development (Frayer, Frederick, & Klausmeier, 1969). The Frayer model is commonly used in

classrooms and helps children develop rich knowledge of an important concept. The students and teacher work together to build a concept by coming up with a definition, characteristics, examples, and nonexamples. Here is a completed Frayer chart for the concept of mammals.

Frayer Model Chart for Mammals

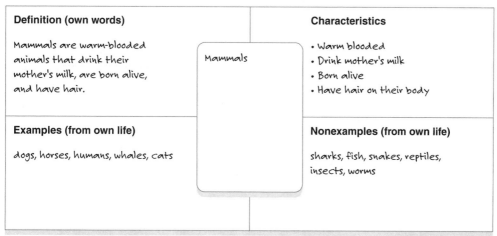

Definition (own words)		Characteristics
Mammals are warm-blooded animals that drink their mother's milk, are born alive, and have hair.	Mammals	• Warm blooded • Drink mother's milk • Born alive • Have hair on their body
Examples (from own life) dogs, horses, humans, whales, cats		**Nonexamples (from own life)** sharks, fish, snakes, reptiles, insects, worms

The reason we think the Frayer model fits well with Thinking Theme lessons is that it includes both examples and nonexamples. Nonexamples demonstrate what a concept is not. Learning what a concept is not strengthens our understanding of what a concept is. We have adapted the Frayer model to build the concept of theme into a framework with six boxes. In a circle in the center, we write the theme word. Later, we will add a kid-friendly definition to this circle. Before reading, we fill in examples and nonexamples from real life and characteristics and noncharacteristics. After reading, we add examples and nonexamples based on the text that's read. Here is how we would introduce the first theme Concept Chart.

If you have used Frayer charts for building concepts in science, math, or social studies, display some of these or remind students what you did. If not, explain to your students that when they are thinking about a concept, it is helpful to come up with both examples and nonexamples of that concept. Tell your students that you are going to build a chart of ideas for the concept of integrity. Display the skeleton chart and write *integrity* in the center. Explain to your students what will be added to the other boxes.

Concept Chart for Integrity

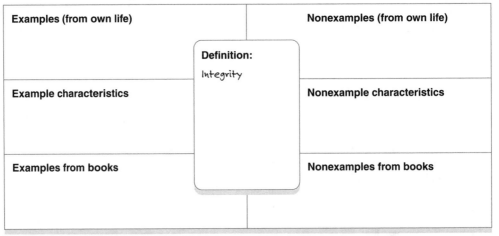

Introduce the chart and the theme you have chosen to work with by saying something like this:

> "Today, we are going to build a Concept Chart for the important life concept of integrity. Our dictionary defines *integrity* as "honesty or sincerity," but you know that we want to come up with our own definition to write in this box. Let's see what we can come up with thinking together about integrity."

Coach your students to come up with an initial definition in their own words. Ask questions such as these:

> "What do you think *integrity* means?"
> "Have you ever heard your mom or dad use the word *integrity*?"

Here are some of the definitions different students came up with:

- "Integrity is being honest, not telling lies."
- "Integrity is doing the right thing even when the people around you are not making the right choices."
- "Integrity is taking responsibility for your actions."
- "Integrity is admitting your mistakes even though you know you might get in trouble for it."
- "Integrity is confessing right away without waiting to be caught by someone."

It is important to elicit a variety of definitions and accept different students' interpretations. One child might think that integrity is taking responsibility for your actions, but another student thinks that integrity is confessing to your mom before she catches you. The idea of offering layers to the definition of the theme allows more students to begin to build their understanding of this important but complex concept.

Next, present three scenarios related to the concept or theme. Relate these scenarios to the school lives all your students share or to your own life, including your own children, friends, and pets. Students are always interested in the "outside school" lives of their teachers, so use this opportunity to let them know that you also struggle with the concept of integrity. Seat your children in talking partners for this activity. After presenting each scenario, have students turn and talk for one minute about the scenario and their opinions about what is right and wrong. Here are some scenarios one teacher used to help students begin their thinking about integrity.

Scenario 1

Your teacher has just assigned a math paper for you to do. Then he leaves the room to see a parent who needs to talk to him right away. All your classmates, including your best friends, start talking and laughing instead of working. You work on your math paper. Someone in the class calls you a "wimp." Are you a wimp, or do you have integrity? Turn and talk to your partner about what you think.

After one minute of talk time, let volunteers tell what they and their partners talked about and decided.

Scenario 2

I am getting food at the drive-through of a local burger joint. I order a burger, fries, and drink. The total for my order comes to $4.55. I give the cashier a $10 bill, and she gives me change back. As I am driving out, I notice she has given me $15.45! The cashier must have thought I gave her a $20 bill! What should I do? Should I go back and return the $10? Do I have integrity if I keep it? No one will ever know, and the cashier was the one who made the mistake. Turn and talk to your partner about what I should do and what this tells you about integrity.

The children are all eager to talk about this—and they have very different opinions. Some are convinced the teacher should go back. Others think that since it wasn't her mistake, she has the right to keep the money. When the talking partner time is up, many students are eager to share their thoughts and opinions. (And they all want to know if this really happened to the teacher and if she went back and returned the money!)

Scenario 3

This is something I actually did when I was about your age. One night, I woke up and I was hungry. I snuck down the stairs and had a bowl of ice cream. I accidentally put the ice cream back in the refrigerator instead of the freezer. The next day, my mom blamed my little sister for making ice-cream "soup" in the middle of the night. I didn't want to get caught. I never confessed. Did I have integrity? What do you think? You have two minutes to talk about this and decide.

Introducing the concept with scenarios children can all relate to and letting them talk to their classmates about each scenario actively engages them in deep thinking. Once children have thought and talked about your scenarios, put them in cooperative groups of three or four and give them six minutes to share their own experiences with integrity. It is important to keep the time for this discussion very short because children will engage in discussion better if they know their time is limited. From our observations, the major reason small-group discussions get off track and create discipline problems is that children say all they have to say quickly and then find other ways to entertain themselves! A timer set for six minutes will keep everyone engaged and on task. It's better for the timer to sound when they are all still actively talking about the concept than to let the discussion go on for too long.

After the small-group discussion, gather children to wherever your Concept Chart is posted, and ask them for examples and nonexamples of integrity. As the children share their experiences, write some of them in the *Examples from own life* box. Stop when you have listed four or five. The purpose is to make the concept of integrity concrete, not to list every example students can think of!

Next, ask if anyone wants to admit to something he or she did that was a nonexample of integrity. Sometimes children are unwilling to admit they have ever been less than honest. If that is the case, list some examples from your own experiences or the experiences of your family. (Make up a few if you can't remember any or are in denial!)

When you have listed four or five examples and nonexamples, help children to come up with the characteristics and noncharacteristics of the concept. These will usually come out of the examples. If children give you more examples when you are trying to get characteristics, turn the example into a characteristic. For instance, if Carl says, "My little brother is always telling lies" when you are trying to get characteristics, write *lying* in the noncharacteristic box.

Once you have filled in these four boxes, create a kid-friendly definition of the concept and write it in the center box. Try to include the ideas expressed by most of your students in their own language for this definition.

Concept Chart for Integrity

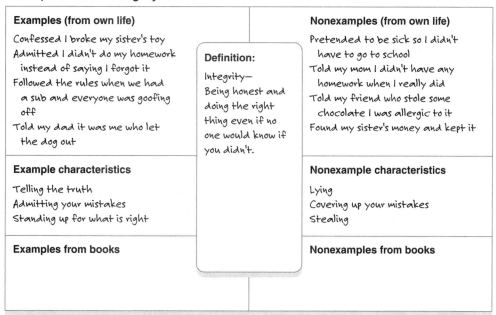

Examples (from own life)

Confessed I broke my sister's toy
Admitted I didn't do my homework
   instead of saying I forgot it
Followed the rules when we had
   a sub and everyone was goofing
   off
Told my dad it was me who let
   the dog out

Definition:

Integrity—
Being honest and
doing the right
thing even if no
one would know if
you didn't.

Nonexamples (from own life)

Pretended to be sick so I didn't
   have to go to school
Told my mom I didn't have any
   homework when I really did
Told my friend who stole some
   chocolate I was allergic to it
Found my sister's money and kept it

Example characteristics

Telling the truth
Admitting your mistakes
Standing up for what is right

Nonexample characteristics

Lying
Covering up your mistakes
Stealing

Examples from books

Nonexamples from books

Your Concept Chart is now complete—except for the examples and nonexamples you will add after reading the story or stories you have chosen for the theme of integrity. You will return to this chart and add those examples and nonexamples when you have completed the Thinking Theme chart and before children write about the theme. Keep the completed chart even after you have added your book examples. You may want to read more stories later in the year in which integrity is the theme. You can use the chart to review the theme before reading the new stories and add information to it when you have finished them. Here is what the chart looked like at the end of the year after children had read *A Day's Work,* by Eve Bunting; *The Summer My Father Was Ten,* by Pat Brisson; and *Too Many Tamales,* by Gary Soto and added examples and nonexamples from these three stories.

Concept Chart for Integrity

Examples (from own life)		Nonexamples (from own life)
Confessed I broke my sister's toy Admitted I didn't do my homework instead of saying I forgot it Followed the rules when we had a sub and everyone was goofing off Told my dad it was me who let the dog out	**Definition:** Integrity— Being honest and doing the right thing even if no one would know if you didn't.	Pretended to be sick so I didn't have to go to school Told my mom I didn't have any homework when I really did Told my friend who stole some chocolate I was allergic to it Found my sister's money and kept it
Example characteristics Telling the truth Admitting your mistakes Standing up for what is right		**Nonexample characteristics** Lying Covering up your mistakes Stealing
Examples from books A Day's Work Abuelo refuses to take money for doing the incorrect work. Abuelo and Grandson redo the work for no pay the next day. The Summer My Father Was Ten My dad helps the man in his garden to repay him for misbehaving. Too Many Tamales Maria confesses to her mother. Maria helps make the second dinner to feed the family.		**Nonexamples from books** A Day's Work Grandson lies to boss that they knew what they were doing in garden. The Summer My Father Was Ten The boys tease the man for being different. Too Many Tamales Maria takes the ring without permission from her mother. Maria and her cousins eat the Christmas dinner while looking for the ring instead of confessing.

To Build a Rich Concept for a Theme

1. Create a Concept Chart with the theme in the center.

2. Tell students that you and they are going to work together to create a chart for the important life concept of _____ (integrity, being a good friend, working hard, perseverance, courage, etc.).

3. Read the dictionary definition of the theme if you like, or give students your own simple definition. Ask what they think the concept means. Do not be surprised or

disheartened if their responses are meager. That just means you really do need to help them build a rich definition. Do not write a definition in the circle yet. Wait until you have completed the examples from life, nonexamples from life, characteristics, and noncharacteristics boxes.

4. Present your class with three scenarios involving the theme. Make these relevant to your own classroom, or present examples from your own experiences. Seat the children in talking partners, and give them one minute to talk about each scenario you present and how it relates to the theme. Let a few volunteers share what they decide through their talking.

5. Put children in groups of three or four to share examples from their own lives. Limit the amount of discussion time to no more than six minutes. Using a timer will help keep everyone on track and create a sense of urgency as the children share their experiences.

6. Gather the class together, and let volunteers share examples from their groups. Write no more than five examples and five nonexamples for the theme. If children are unwilling to volunteer nonexamples, add some from your life experiences.

7. Add three or four characteristics and noncharacteristics to the chart. If children continue to give you examples, turn the example into a characteristic.

8. Write a kid-friendly definition for the concept in the center circle.

9. After reading the selection or selections based on the theme, add more examples and nonexamples from the selections.

10. Keep the chart to review the theme if you choose to read stories with this theme later in the year. Add more examples based on these new selections.

Linking Characters to Theme

I f the *theme* is the big idea that a story is about, then the *characters* are what give life to that theme. In a well-crafted story, characters change from the beginning of the story to the end of the story. Watching the characters grow and change is a big part of what makes a story interesting to us, the readers. When we talk about a book with friends or describe a book as a "great" book, we often also talk about the characters and how they grow and change. Analyzing what characters do and say and how they interact is the key to helping students think about the theme.

Finding out about characters is mostly a matter of paying attention to the details the author gives us about characters. We tell students that it is our job as readers to be detectives and figure out what the author is trying to tell us about each character. We do this by paying attention to what characters say and do and thinking about what these words and actions tell us. Is the character full of pride? A tattletale? A generous soul?

We tell students that a clever author slips the character's thoughts and feelings into descriptions and dialogues instead of just blatantly stating "Little Joyce is jealous of her baby sister." By paying attention to the interactions between characters and observing how characters grow and change in a story, we can often understand the theme.

We teach students to link characters to theme by leading them to think about what the character does, why the character acts that way, what the character might get out of doing this, and whether this action is an example or nonexample of the theme. We chart characters' actions linked to theme on a Thinking Theme Chart.

Thinking Theme Chart Skeleton

Big Question:			
Event or **actions** by characters connected to the theme, including examples and nonexamples	**Why** does the character act this way?	What does the character **get** for acting this way?	Does this event show the **theme** of _____ ? Yes, because *or* No, because

To teach students the kind of thinking we want them to do when we are linking characters with theme, we start with a story that is very familiar to our students—one they have read or heard many times. We pose the big question and read aloud the story, stopping at each key point where there is an event that clearly says something about the theme. We list that event in the first column of the chart and then lead children to answer the **Why, Get,** and **Theme** questions in the next three columns. We listen to several children's thinking before capturing the consensus of the group and recording it on the chart.

Here is an example lesson based on the familiar story *The Little Engine That Could,* by Watty Piper, that will work with any elementary classroom. The major theme of this story is perseverance. The toys have perseverance, since they do not give up trying to get to the children even after their train engine breaks down and several passing engines refuse their request for help. Having perseverance is a theme children can relate to when it is put in kid-friendly language.

The teacher begins the lesson by asking students if anyone knows what *perseverance* means and accepting their responses. After refusing to see any hands until thirty seconds of "think time" has passed, she gets a variety of responses from the children about perseverance:

> **Michael:** I think that it means working and working and working until you know something.
>
> **Susie:** Perseverance is trying until you get it right.
>
> **Daniel:** It is never giving up.

Together, they come up with a tentative definition for *perseverance*—not giving up, no matter how tough it gets. The teacher reminds the children that they will expand this definition as they think about experiences they have had with perseverance and read a story in which perseverance is the theme, or big idea.

Next, the teacher presents three scenarios in which perseverance is needed to accomplish the goal. After each scenario, the children work as talking partners to discuss what that scenario tells them about perseverance. Next the children meet for six minutes in groups of three or four and talk about times in their lives when they and their friends have shown perseverance or perhaps given up. When the six minutes is up, the teacher gathers the group together and they construct this Concept Chart for perseverance.

Concept Chart for Perseverance

Examples (from own life)	Definition:	Nonexamples (from own life)
Kept looking for something I lost until I found it Kept practicing my piano piece until I could play it perfectly Kept practicing my jump shot until I could get the ball in Practiced the multiplication tables until I learned them	Perseverance— to keep trying and trying different things until you succeed; never giving up	Quit music lessons because they were too hard Dad gave up on his diet Mom quit trying to make me clean up my room Quit trying to teach my dog tricks
Example characteristics Keep trying even if it is hard Practice until you get it Believe you can do it and you can		**Nonexample characteristics** Giving up Quitting when something is hard Not working hard enough
Examples from books		**Nonexamples from books**

Next the teacher shows students the familiar book *The Little Engine That Could.* Most of them know the story and are delighted to see it again. The teacher lets them share their fond memories of the book and then says,

"I am going to read this book to you, and I want you to think about how the toys show perseverance. As you listen to me read, I want you to think about this big question."

She points to the big question at the top of the Thinking Theme Chart and has the children read it with her:

Big Question: "Sometimes people do not give up, no matter how tough it gets. What are some ways that having perseverance is helpful or useful to the toys?"

Thinking Theme Chart for Perseverance

Big Question: Sometimes people do not give up, no matter how tough it gets. What are some ways that having perseverance is helpful or useful to the toys?			
Event or **actions** by characters connected to the theme, including examples and nonexamples	**Why** does the character act this way?	What does the character **get** for acting this way?	Does this event show the **theme** of perseverance? Yes, because *or* No, because

The teacher explains that to answer the big question, students are going to have to do some really deep thinking about the characters. They are going to think about what the characters do. But more important, they are going to try to decide why the characters act as they do, what they might get out of acting that way, and what their actions say about the theme of perseverance. The teacher then points to the heading of the first column on the chart and has the students read it with her:

"*Events* or *actions* by characters connected to the theme, including examples and nonexamples."

Linking Characters to Theme

She explains,

> "The first column is where we will list events and actions that we think relate to the theme of perseverance. Today we are going to follow the decisions the toys make that tell us something about their perseverance. Just as when we made our perseverance Concept Chart, we are looking for both examples and nonexamples of the toys and their perseverance. I am going to read the book to you, stopping several times and asking you to think about an event or action the toys do."

The teacher directs the children's attention back to the Thinking Theme Chart, and they read the heading for the second column together:

> "*Why* does the character act this way?"

The teacher helps students understand that this is where they are going to have to do some deep thinking to try to figure out why the toys did what they did. Together, the teacher and students read the question in the third column:

> "What does the character *get* for acting this way?"

The children understand that they are to do some deep thinking to try to figure out what the toys get from their action. They read the heading for the last column, and the teacher reminds them that they can't just say yes or no. They have to provide reasons for their answers. The teacher asks,

> "Does this event show the *theme* of perseverance?
>
> > Yes, because . . .
> >
> > No, because . . ."

Before reading the first section of the story to students, the teacher makes clear their purpose for listening by pointing to the key words in the columns—**events** or **actions, why, get,** and **theme**—as she says,

> "Your job today is to think about *actions* the toys do, *why* they might do them, what they *get* out of doing them, and what their actions tell us about our *theme* of perseverance."

The teacher then reads the first part of the story, in which the original engine breaks down and the shiny passenger engine refuses his request to pull him over the mountain. The teacher has placed a sticky flag at the bottom of the page on which she wants to stop for the first discussion. She points to this sticky flag and tells students,

"This sticky flag means *stop, think,* and *talk.*"

Stop and think!

Turning to the Thinking Theme Chart the teacher says,

"The first event I want us to discuss today is when the toys are stranded and ask the shiny passenger engine for a ride. I think that event tells us something about perseverance, so I am going to write it in this first column."

The teacher then points to the second column and asks students to turn to their talking partners and discuss why they think the toys ask the shiny engine for a ride. After students have had a chance to share their thinking with their partners, she asks volunteers to share their thinking:

Carl: They had to ask for help so they could get to the children.

Maria: I think the toys could have just sat and done nothing but they didn't.

Andrew: It is hard to ask for help when you don't know if someone might laugh at you.

Maria: The engine did laugh at the toys!

David: It must have been hard for the toys to ask for help again.

After the teacher listens to several explanations of why the toys ask the engine for a ride, she then records a few phrases in column two, capturing the essence of students' ideas.

The teacher then directs the students to turn their attention to the third column and asks them to talk with their partners about what the toys get out of asking the shiny new engine for help. Again, the teacher follows the turn-and-talk time with a whole-class discussion. She asks,

"What do you think the toys get when they ask the shiny engine for help?"

The students think for a minute, and then Andrew answers, "The toys were rejected." The teacher encourages him to justify his thinking by asking "Why did you say that?" This generates more responses:

Andrew: The engine wouldn't stop, so that is why we decided the toys were rejected.

Sarah: Emily and I thought the toys got a big sigh. You know how you sigh when someone doesn't do what you want? We think the toys sighed!

Teacher: Any other ideas?

John [quietly]: Wind in their face.

Maria: That's right. When the train does not pick up the toys and just takes off down the track, the wind probably blows in their face, like when we stand by the train tracks.

The teacher comments that they probably did indeed get wind in their faces and records their ideas in column three. Next, she points to the fourth column and says that students' final thinking task for this event is to decide if the event is a good example of the theme—perseverance: "Do you think the toys show perseverance in asking the shiny engine? Talk with your partner, and remember that you need a reason for answering yes or no." Again, the children discuss with their talking partners, and then volunteers share their thoughts with the whole class. Roberto says he doesn't think the story is about perseverance. The teacher encourages him to dig deeper.

Teacher: Roberto, what is your support for that thinking? Please give a reason. [Sarah starts to answer, saying that she agrees with Roberto. The teacher smiles at Sarah, but quickly intervenes.] Sarah, let Roberto finish his thinking, unless he asks for someone else's help. [The teacher gently but firmly reminds Roberto what he was saying before Sarah wanted to help.] Roberto, you don't think it is perseverance because . . .

Roberto: I do *not* think it is perseverance because the toys asked the shiny engine only one time. Perseverance would be asking over and over and over and over and over, not just once.

Ramon: They didn't have a chance to ask over and over. That mean engine just laughed at them and took off.

Sarah: But they could have yelled and tried to get him to change his mind.

The teacher comments that both ways of thinking make sense to her, and she records both the yes and no responses along with students' reasons in the fourth column.

. . . .

43

Thinking Theme Chart for Perseverance: One Event Filled In

Big Question: Sometimes people do not give up, no matter how tough it gets. What are some ways that having perseverance is helpful or useful to the toys?			
Event or **actions** by characters connected to the theme, including examples and nonexamples	**Why** does the character act this way?	What does the character **get** for acting this way?	Does this event show the **theme** of perseverance? Yes, because *or* No, because
The toys ask the shiny passenger engine for a ride.	Their engine breaks down. They need an engine to pull them. They want to get to the kids.	They are laughed at and rejected. They feel the wind in their faces.	No, because the toys only ask one time. Yes, because they ask and don't just give up when their engine breaks down.

The teacher continues reading the book until she comes to the second sticky flag, which she has placed at the point in the story where both the freight engine and the rusty old engine refuse to help. The teacher says that the next event they will discuss is the toys' asking two more trains to help them. She writes "The toys ask two more trains to help" in the **Event** column. Next, she points to the second column and says,

Stop and think!

> "Our next step is thinking about why did the toys behave that way. Talk with your partner about why you think the toys did this."

Here's the conversation between students in one partnership:

Rebecca: The toys still want to get to the kids.

Michael: Their train is broken, so they need a ride.

Rebecca: They had to keep asking until they got a yes.

Michael: They are getting pretty discouraged though. They probably think no engine will help them.

After listening to several partnerships, the teacher has all the students direct their attention to her and the Thinking Theme Chart. Volunteers share what their partnerships discussed, and the teacher records a few ideas in the second column.

The teacher directs the students' attention to the third column. She has the children read the column heading with her, and then they quickly turn and talk about what they think the toys get out of asking the freight engine and the rusty old engine for help. Volunteers share what their partnerships discussed, and the teacher records a few phrases in column three, capturing their ideas.

As the teacher points to the fourth column, the children are obviously eager to talk with their partners and express their opinions. They all seem to agree that the toys show perseverance because they ask three different trains for help and don't just give up.

Jamarcio: I think yes because they asked every train that came along.

Meghan: I agree. That is perseverance—trying and trying and trying and trying and trying!

The teacher records their unanimous yes in the fourth column on the chart.

Thinking Theme Chart for Perseverance: Two Events Filled In

Big Question:			
Sometimes people do not give up, no matter how tough it gets. What are some ways that having perseverance is helpful or useful to the toys?			
Event or **actions** by characters connected to the theme, including examples and nonexamples	**Why** does the character act this way?	What does the character **get** for acting this way?	Does this event show the **theme** of perseverance? Yes, because *or* No, because
The toys ask the shiny passenger engine for a ride.	Their engine breaks down. They need an engine to pull them. They want to get to the kids.	They are laughed at and rejected. They feel the wind in their faces.	No, because the toys only ask one time. Yes, because they ask and don't just give up when their engine breaks down.
They ask the freight engine and the rusty old engine to pull them.	They still want to get to the kids. They think some engine will be kind and help them.	They get "no" for the answer. They get very sad. They almost cry.	Yes, because the toys keep asking over and over and over.

The teacher continues reading to the end of the book. Even though most of the children know the story and that it is going to turn out all right, their delight is apparent when the little blue engine agrees to try and successfully pulls the train full of toys over the mountain. After giving the children a few minutes to savor the victory, the teacher writes the last event she wants to discuss on the chart.

The toys convince the little blue engine to try.

After writing this on the chart, she says,

"The last event that I want us to discuss today is when the toys convince the little blue train to try. This time, talk about all the questions with your partners. Then we will come back and have a class discussion. Your job with this event is to think about why the characters act this way, what they get out of acting this way, and what this action tells us about the theme."

One of the partnerships has this conversation:

Maria: OK, the first question we talk about is **why** do the toys ask the little blue engine to help?

Andrew: The toys need help and don't give up asking.

Maria: And the little blue engine doesn't give up either.

Andrew: OK, so the next question we have to discuss is what do the toys **get** for acting this way? What do the toys **get** because they keep trying?

Maria: That's easy. They get over the mountain! They get to the kids.

Andrew: That's right, and I think yes is the answer to the last question.

Maria: I agree, but we can't just say yes. We have to tell why we think so.

Andrew: It's yes because they keep trying and trying until the toys get to the children. The toys never give up. That is perseverance.

Once again, the class is unanimous in their opinion that the toys show perseverance in asking the little blue engine for help, even though they are rejected three times. The teacher records their responses on the chart and congratulates them on the deep thinking they have done about the characters and about the big idea of perseverance.

Thinking Theme Chart for Perseverance: Completed

Big Question:			
Sometimes people do not give up, no matter how tough it gets. What are some ways that having perseverance is helpful or useful to the toys?			
Event or **actions** by characters connected to the theme, including examples and nonexamples	**Why** does the character act this way?	What does the character **get** for acting this way?	Does this event show the **theme** of perseverance? Yes, because or No, because
The toys ask the shiny passenger engine for a ride.	Their engine breaks down. They need an engine to pull them. They want to get to the kids.	They are laughed at and rejected. They feel the wind in their faces.	No, because the toys only ask one time. Yes, because they ask and don't just give up when their engine breaks down.
They ask the freight engine and the rusty old engine to pull them.	They still want to get to the kids. They think some engine will be kind and help them.	They get "no" for the answer. They get very sad. They almost cry.	Yes, because the toys keep asking over and over and over.
The toys convince the little blue engine to try.	They need help. They don't give up. The little blue engine is kind and asks what their problem is.	They get over the mountain and get to the kids! They prove to the little engine that he can do it if he tries.	Yes, because they keep trying even when they know it would be hard for the little engine to do it.

Next, she has students read the big question with her once again:

Big Question: "Sometimes people do not give up, no matter how tough it gets. What are some ways that having perseverance is helpful or useful to the toys?"

The children talk one final time with their partners and conclude that having perseverance is very useful to the toys because they would never have reached the children if they had just given up.

The teacher ends the lesson by turning the children's attention back to the perseverance Concept Chart:

"Are there any examples or nonexamples of perseverance from *The Little Engine That Could* that we should add to the chart?

The children decide they should add the toys' continuing to ask for help until they get it to the *Examples* box. Since they still can't decide if the toys' asking the first train for help is an example or nonexample of perseverance, nothing is added to the *Nonexample* box. The teacher tells the children she will save this chart because they will be reading other stories in which perseverance is an important theme and they will add more examples and maybe even some nonexamples from these stories. The students all appear pleased with themselves, and the teacher knows they will be glad to revisit the concept of perseverance when they read the books *Uncle Jed's Barbershop,* by Margaree King Mitchell; *Baseball Saved Us,* by Ken Mochizuki; and *Sarah, Plain and Tall,* by Patricia MacLachlan.

Concept Chart for Perseverance: Completed

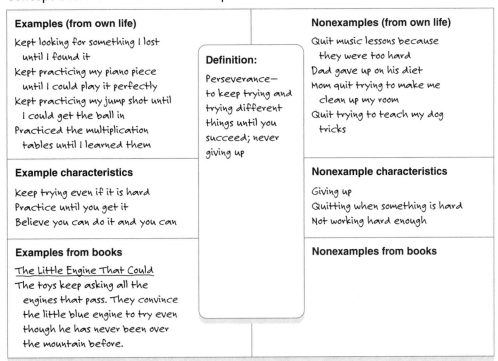

Examples (from own life)

Kept looking for something I lost until I found it

Kept practicing my piano piece until I could play it perfectly

Kept practicing my jump shot until I could get the ball in

Practiced the multiplication tables until I learned them

Definition:

Perseverance—to keep trying and trying different things until you succeed; never giving up

Nonexamples (from own life)

Quit music lessons because they were too hard

Dad gave up on his diet

Mom quit trying to make me clean up my room

Quit trying to teach my dog tricks

Example characteristics

Keep trying even if it is hard

Practice until you get it

Believe you can do it and you can

Nonexample characteristics

Giving up

Quitting when something is hard

Not working hard enough

Examples from books

The Little Engine That Could

The toys keep asking all the engines that pass. They convince the little blue engine to try even though he has never been over the mountain before.

Nonexamples from books

To help children learn how to analyze characters' actions and relate them to a theme, teachers often choose a story that is well known to their students. This allows the children to concentrate all their attention on learning how to think about the theme, since they already know the retelling details of the story. The lesson is usually done in a read-aloud fashion so that the children do not need to juggle the two tasks of decoding and thinking. The teacher usually chooses the events students should think about. The students' job is to think about why the characters act this way, what they get out of acting this way, and what this action tells about the theme. Once children understand the kind of thinking they need to do in a Thinking Theme lesson, the teacher turns over to them the responsibility for choosing the events as well as deciding why the events happen, what the characters get from the events, and what the events tell about the characters and the theme.

To Teach Children How to Think about Characters and Theme

1. Choose a story with a strong theme that is familiar to students so they can concentrate all their attention on thinking about the theme.
2. Seat children in talking partners.
3. Build a Concept Chart for the theme you have chosen.
4. Show the children the Thinking Theme Chart, and have them read the big question with you.
5. Have students read the headings in all four columns, and help them understand that their job is to think about why characters do certain actions, what they might get out of doing these actions, and what these actions show about the characters and the theme.
6. Seat children in talking partners, and read aloud to them until you reach the first sticky flag you have placed at the first *stop, talk,* and *think* place.
7. When you get to the first sticky flag, write the event you have chosen, because it relates to the theme in the first column.
8. Have the children read the heading of the second column and then turn and talk about **why** they think that event occurred.
9. Let volunteers share their thinking, and record their ideas in column two.
10. Have the children read the heading of the third column and then turn and talk about what the characters might **get** out of that action.
11. Let volunteers share their thinking, and record their ideas in column three.
12. Have the children read the heading of the fourth column and then turn and talk about whether they think the event is an example or nonexample of the **theme.**

13. Let volunteers share their thinking, and record their ideas in column four. If they disagree but can support both sides, write both the yes and the no along with their reasons.

14. Continue this procedure of reading to students, stopping at a sticky flag, and writing an event in column one and having children share their thinking first with partners and then with the whole class to complete the chart. For the first lesson, limit the number of events or actions to three or four.

15. Direct students' attention back to the big question. Have them talk about this with their talking partners and then share with the whole class.

16. Add examples and nonexamples from the story to your Concept Chart. Tell students you will save the chart, because they will be thinking about this theme in other stories throughout the year.

Teaching Children to Write Responses about Characters and Themes

nce our students understand how to think about characters and themes, we want them to learn how to construct written responses sharing their opinions and supporting them with details from the story. As with all new things we want students to learn, we carefully scaffold this instruction so that everyone can succeed. We use a model of gradual release of responsibility, in which we do much of the work the first several times and gradually turn over the responsibility to our students.

In this chapter, we demonstrate how one teacher teaches students to write a written response to a theme question. First, the teacher has the students write a personal choice response on a real-life topic of interest to all of them. Next, they learn to construct a theme response based on one story. Finally, the teacher builds on students' ability to compose a

written response to one text to help them learn to compose a written response to two texts that share a theme.

Throughout this book, we have tried to embody the principle that when you are teaching something new, your students will have greater success if you use a familiar topic. Doing so allows students to concentrate all their energy on the new skill. In this chapter, we begin teaching students how to write a response based on personal choice and to support that choice with details about real-life, kid-friendly choices about a topic such as food, sports, or school specials. Once they have written one or more personal choice responses, they will transfer what they have learned to writing responses relating characters' actions to themes.

Learning to Write a Personal Choice Response

The teacher begins the lesson by asking some simple real-life questions and teaching students to turn the questions into statements by deleting words they don't need and adding words they do. The question always asks for an opinion. Here is a question many students enjoy answering:

Do you like ice cream or cookies for dessert?

The teacher has the children indicate which they would choose and then moves all the "cookies people" to one side of the room and all the "ice cream people" to the other side. Starting with the people who chose ice cream, the teacher asks them to think about a sentence they could write that would tell that they had chosen ice cream. The "cookies people" watch as the teacher and the "ice cream people" decide what words they need to clearly state their choice. The teacher crosses out and erases unneeded words and adds words as needed. Here's the first question the students write:

Do you like ice cream or cookies for dessert?

The students who chose ice cream read the sentence and decide they don't need the word *cookies,* since they are the ice cream group. The teacher erases the word *cookies.*

Do you like ice cream or   for dessert?

The teacher and children read the sentence again. Now the children decide that they don't need *or,* so *or* is erased.

Do you like ice cream   for dessert?

The teacher reads the words that are left and tells the children there is at least one more word they don't need. It takes a little thinking time, but someone finally says the word *you*. The teacher says, "Right!" He explains that the question is asking for someone's opinion, but to answer the question, that person doesn't need the word *you*. *You* is erased, leaving this:

> Do like ice cream   for dessert?

Next, the teacher asks if any more words can be erased. The children don't see any more unneeded words, but one child suggests that that the question mark isn't needed, since they are answering the question, not asking it. The teacher remarks that he hadn't thought of it but that the student is right. He erases the question mark:

> Do like ice cream   for dessert

Now the teacher asks, "Do we need to add any words to write a clear sentence that states our choice for dessert?" The children immediately see that the word *I* is needed, and the teacher adds it but in the wrong place:

> Do like ice cream   for dessert I

The teacher and children read the words and all construct a sentence that uses all the words:

> I do like ice cream for dessert.

Several children think this doesn't sound right—that what someone would really say is "I like ice cream for dessert." The teacher agrees, and the sentence clearly stating their choice is done:

> I like ice cream for dessert.

Meanwhile, the "cookies people" have been observing. The teacher now takes them through the same process, but this time, he lets the students take the lead. The question is once again written:

> Do you like ice cream or cookies for dessert?

Volunteers are asked to come and erase words. *Ice cream, or, you, do,* and the *?* are quickly erased, and the students construct this sentence:

> I like cookies for dessert.

Next, the teacher hands everyone a piece of paper on which this question is written:

Is basketball, football, soccer, or baseball your favorite sport?

The children read the sentence, and the teacher tells them that they are going to turn that question into a clear statement of choice by crossing out unneeded words, adding words that are needed, and constructing a good sentence with those words. He has each child indicate his or her favorite sport, and creates "teams" according to students' choices. Eight children have chosen football, and after deciding that that is too large a group to work together, the teacher forms two football teams. He appoints a "coach" for each team and sends the children to different places in the room, giving them four minutes to cross out and add words and construct a clear sentence stating their choice. The children quickly get into their teams and the teacher circulates, helping the teams as necessary. The children quickly reassemble and read their clear statements of choice. These simple sentences all follow the same general pattern, except that some children chose to write a group response and others interpreted the question to ask for their individual responses. The teacher assures the students that both ways of writing the sentence are fine, since they wrote it as a group but made the choice as individuals. Here are the groups' sentences:

Soccer is our favorite sport.
Baseball is my favorite sport.
Football is our favorite sport.
Basketball is our favorite sport.

Next, the teacher gives everyone a piece of paper on which another question is written:

Is your favorite special art, music, or P.E.?

He asks the children individually to construct their response by crossing out and adding words. The children quickly do so and construct their own clear responses. P.E. wins, but many children have chosen art and music. Some children have begun their sentences with the name of the special; other children have ended their sentences with their choice. The teacher assures them that both ways of writing the sentence are clear and correct:

P.E. is my favorite special.
My favorite special is art.

Next the teacher puts the art, music, and P.E. people in groups and has the groups brainstorm reasons for choosing the special they did. A recorder in each group lists their reasons on a chart. When the charts have been completed, each child uses the information on it to write a paragraph that begins with the sentence stating his or her choice and includes other sentences that give specific reasons and details for that choice.

P.E. Reasons Chart

Loud	Don't have to walk in quiet straight lines	Fun
Get sweaty	Play different games	Play with friends
Exercise	Run around	Different teacher

Miguel looked at the words generated by the P.E. group and wrote this paragraph:

P.E is my favorite special. I don't have to walk in quiet straight lines. I play all kinds of games with my friends. We get sweaty and run around the gym. It is great fun to have a different teacher for class. We are loud and get lots of exercise. I look forward to P.E. all day.

When the children have written their responses, the teacher shows them a checklist they will use to evaluate their responses. He leads the children through each point on the checklist by checking it against the paragraph just written, demonstrating how to mark each item correctly done.

Checklist for Choice Response

❑ 1. Do I take a position and clearly answer the question?

❑ 2. Do I support my answer with specific examples and details?

❑ 3. Is my response complete?

The teacher says,

"Read your first sentence. I know you have all clearly stated your favorite special, so you can give yourself a check for number 1. For number 2, ask yourself if you have included specific examples and details to support your choice. Give yourself a check if you have. Question 3 asks you to think about whether your answer is complete. Have you included enough details and examples to explain your choice of favorite special? Give yourself a check if you think you have enough details and examples. If you don't think you have enough, add one more."

Not all students will need the explicit instruction provided in this example. Nonetheless, the whole lesson, as just described, takes less than an hour, and presenting it like this will ensure that all your students will understand what you want them to do when writing personal choice responses. Because of the scaffolding provided in the lesson, all students will be successful in writing their responses and will carry this expectation of success into the next and more difficult task of writing a theme response.

Constructing a Written Response on the Theme of One Selection

The teacher begins teaching students to write a theme response by using a selection for which the children have completed the theme Concept Chart and the Thinking Theme Chart. He has the children turn their attention to the big question that they have been answering orally and tells them that they will now learn how to write an answer to that question. He then shows them the checklist he will use to make sure they have answered the question clearly and completely.

Thinking Theme Checklist for One Text

❑ 1. Do I take a position and clearly answer the question?

❑ 2. Do I include my definition of the theme?

❑ 3. Do I support my answer with specific examples and details from the selection?

❑ 4. Is my response complete?

The teacher reminds students of how they learned to state their opinions clearly by using some words from the question and adding other words they needed. He displays the problem-solving Concept Chart and Thinking Theme Chart based on *Buzzy the Bumblebee,* by Denise Brennan-Nelson. The teacher has the children read the big question:

Buzzy has one big problem and many small problems to solve. Do you think Buzzy is a good problem solver?

The teacher gives everyone thirty seconds to think about how to begin writing his or her response by clearly stating an opinion. The teacher then asks students to suggest words they won't need for their first sentence, and he erases those unneeded words. Someone suggests they don't need the whole first sentence. Everyone agrees, so the first sentence is erased:

Do you think Buzzy is a good problem solver?

Students are eager to suggest that both *you* and the *?* should be erased, and they are:

Do   think Buzzy is a good problem solver

To the question of what important word needs to be added, the students quickly respond *I*. The teacher adds *I* at the end:

Do   think Buzzy is a good problem solver   I

Next the teacher asks students to tell what the first sentence could now say, and they respond:

I think Buzzy is a good problem solver.

The teacher helps them notice that they do not need the word *do,* although including it also makes a good, clear first sentence:

I do think Buzzy is a good problem solver.

Next, the teacher points out that while most students will agree that Buzzy is a good problem solver, some might disagree. How would they write their first sentence? The children quickly realize that the word *not* is needed and that it can go in two places:

I do not think Buzzy is a good problem solver.
I think Buzzy is not a good problem solver.

The teacher has all the children take out their reading-response notebooks and write the sentences that state their opinions. He tells them that they are going to write paragraphs explaining their reasons, so he asks everyone to indent the first sentence.

Once everyone has written this first sentence, the teacher tells them that "The next thing we need to do is to make sure our reader knows what we mean by *solving problems.*" The teacher has students review the information recorded on the problem-solving Concept Chart and then asks each student to write a sentence telling what problem solving means to him or her.

Concept Chart for Problem Solving

Examples (from own life)
 	
Put things away or locked them up
Helped my sister fix broken toy
Talked about friend's hurt
  feelings and apologized to her
	Nonexamples (from own life)
	
	Didn't listen to my dad
	Ignored someone who fell down
	  Would not give the little boy a
	  bandage
	Teased the other girls in the
	  classroom

Example characteristics
 	
Helping other people with stuff
Fixing things that break
Talking about a problem with
  the person causing it
Figuring out what is wrong
  and fixing it
	Nonexample characteristics
	
	Ignoring the problem
	Arguing, disagreeing
	Walking away instead of helping

Examples from books Buzzy figures out how to climb down from the plant, even though he has never done it before. Buzzy makes a boat from a feather to float across the stream. Buzzy realizes he couldn't fly because he lost confidence in his ability to fly.	**Nonexamples from books** Buzzy does not fly home after reading the book because he believes the book and not in himself and his ability to fly.

Definition:

Problem Solving—using your own brain and help from other people to solve a problem or fix something

The teacher observes students looking at the Concept Chart, remembering the kid-friendly definition of the theme and the problem-solving characteristics. When they have all written their definition sentences, he asks several children to share their sentences:

> Problem solving is fixing something with your brain.
> Problem solving is figuring out what to do when you have never done it before.
> Problem solving is getting help from other people who know more.

Next, the teacher has the children look at the Thinking Theme Chart, and together they review the events they chose that tell something about a character and the theme. Together, they read each event and what they recorded in the **Why, Get,** and **Theme** columns.

Constructing a Written Response on the Theme of One Selection

Thinking Theme Chart for Problem Solving

Big Question:
Buzzy has one big problem and many small problems to solve.
Do you think Buzzy is a good problem solver?

Event or **actions** by characters connected to the theme, including examples and nonexamples	**Why** does the character act this way?	What does the character **get** for acting this way?	Does this event show the **theme** of problem solving? Yes, because or No, because
Buzzy reads that bees can't fly.	He likes to read and usually believes what he reads.	He is confused and unhappy. He used to fly, but now he is convinced that he can't.	This is the start of the problem Buzzy has to solve.
Buzzy climbs down from the flower.	He has to get down, and he thinks he can't fly.	He gets down, but he almost slips and falls.	Yes, because he doesn't stay up there the rest of his life.
Buzzy asks the dragonflies to walk with him.	He is scared and lonely.	He is envious and mad that the dragonflies won't walk with him.	Yes, because he is trying to get help to solve his problems.
Buzzy trudges through the grass, trying to get home to his family.	He doesn't think he can fly, and he has to get home.	He is tired and worried he will never be able to fly again.	Yes, he needs to get home so walking works.
Buzzy makes a boat from a feather and floats home.	He has to cross the stream and he can't swim.	He is joyful and relieved.	Yes, he is still heading home.
Buzzy runs the rest of the way home through the tall grass.	He is afraid, alone, and worried.	He is tired.	Yes, he is still heading home.
Buzzy realizes he can fly after talking to his parents.	His parents tell him to believe in himself.	He has the confidence to fly. He is proud that he solved the problem of how to get home. He realizes he shouldn't believe everything he reads; he should use common sense, too.	Yes, he solved his problem because now he can fly again.

The teacher chooses one event from the chart and models for students how to write sentences, showing how this relates to the theme:

> "I am going to write about how Buzzy asks the dragonflies for help. Watch how I include his asking, why he asked, what he gets out of asking, and how this shows he is a good problem solver."

As the children watch, the teacher writes:

> Buzzy is afraid, and so he asks the dragonflies to walk with him. They don't and it makes him mad. Even though it doesn't work, asking the dragonflies for help shows good problem solving because asking for help is one way we solve problems.

After the teacher has written these sentences, he has the students read them with him and explains how he very cleverly included the following information:

- The **why**—he is afraid
- The **get**—it doesn't work
- The **theme** connection—asking for help is one way we solve problems

Next the teacher asks everyone to choose one event (any one except the dragonflies) and write sentences explaining what Buzzy does, why he does it, and how it shows he is (or isn't) a good problem solver. As the children write, they look up at the Thinking Theme Chart, obviously thinking about how to include information from all four columns. The teacher goes over to two students who are clearly struggling and coaches them one on one to construct their sentences. When everyone has written something, the teacher asks several children to share their responses. When a student has not used information from one of the columns, everyone helps him or her think about how to add that information. Here are some of the responses students wrote:

> I think Buzzy is a good problem solver. Problem solving is getting help from other people who know more. Buzzy does not think he can fly until his parents talk to him and remind him to believe in himself. Buzzy decides not to believe everything that he reads in books is true. He has solved his problem because he now has the confidence to fly again.

I do think Buzzy is a good problem solver. Problem solving is figuring out how to do something you have never done before. Buzzy makes a boat from a feather so he can get across the stream. He is relieved when he gets across the stream, and this helps him get home.

I think Buzzy is a good problem solver. Problem solving is figuring out how to do something you have never done before. He climbs down from the flower. He has to because he can't fly. He almost slips, but he does get down and doesn't stay up there for the rest of his life.

Once the students have listened to several children share their responses and helped fix responses that don't include information from all four columns, the teacher puts them in partners to revise their own writing. The partners read each other's response and give what help they can to make sure information from all four columns is included. The teacher has partnered the two struggling students and works with them to make their responses more complete.

Finally, the teacher asks the students to choose one more event from the story and write about it, including information from all four columns. The children find this relatively easy since they have all heard many different events described by other students. Here are the final papers of the three students shown earlier:

I think Buzzy is a good problem solver. Problem solving is getting help from other people who know more. Buzzy does not think he can fly until his parents talk to him and remind him to believe in himself. Buzzy decides not to believe everything that he reads in books is true. He has solved his problem because he now has the confidence to fly again. Buzzy also is a good problem solver when he makes the boat. He has to get across the stream, and he doesn't know how to swim. He is joyful and relieved, and I think it helps his confidence.

I do think Buzzy is a good problem solver. Problem solving is figuring out how to do something you have never done before. Buzzy makes a boat from a feather so he can get across the stream. He is relieved when he gets across the stream, and this helps him get home. Buzzy runs though the tall grass. He is afraid and alone and tired, but he runs anyway and is almost home.

I think Buzzy is a good problem solver. Problem solving is figuring out how to do something you have never done before. He climbs down from the flower. He has to because he can't fly. He almost slips, but he does get down and doesn't stay up there for the rest of his life. Buzzy makes a boat because he can't swim. He gets across the stream and is relieved to be on his way home. Making the boat is good problem solving. He probably has never ever made a boat before.

After the students have completed their responses, they evaluate them using the Thinking Theme Checklist for One Text. The teacher also evaluates them using this checklist, and the following day, he pulls together a small group of children who need to revise their papers so that they can get four checks.

Thinking Theme Checklist for One Text

❑ 1. Do I take a position and clearly answer the question?

❑ 2. Do I include my definition of the theme?

❑ 3. Do I support my answer with specific examples and details from the selection?

❑ 4. Is my response complete?

Constructing a Written Response on Theme for Two Selections

Once the students have learned to write about the theme in one text, it is relatively easy to help them transfer that knowledge to writing about the same theme in two texts. In this lesson, the teacher follows the previous lesson about Buzzy's problem solving by reminding students of another story they read in which problem solving was the theme, "A Swim" in *Frog and Toad Are Friends*. They revisit the Thinking Theme Chart they completed for "A Swim."

Thinking Theme Chart for Problem Solving

Big Question:			
Toad has a problem. How well do you think he solves his problem?			
Event or **actions** by characters connected to the theme, including examples and nonexamples	**Why** does the character act this way?	What does the character **get** for acting this way?	Does this event show the **theme** of problem solving? Yes, because or No, because
Toad tells Frog not to look at him until he gets in the water.	He thinks he looks funny in his bathing suit.	Toad gets what he wanted. Frog doesn't see his bathing suit.	Yes, he doesn't want Frog to see his bathing suit and Frog doesn't.
Toad asks Frog to tell Turtle to go away.	He doesn't want Turtle to see his bathing suit.	Nothing. Turtle won't go.	No, because Turtle won't leave.
Toad waits in the water for all the animals to leave.	He doesn't want anyone to see him in his bathing suit.	He is cold and shivering.	No, because the animals don't leave.
Toad gets out of the water.	He is cold and has to get out to go home.	All the animals laugh at him.	No, because all the animals see him in his bathing suit.

Now, the teacher poses a new question based on the two stories, *Buzzy the Bumblebee* and "A Swim" in *Frog and Toad Are Friends:*

Buzzy and Toad both have problems to solve. Buzzy solves his problem, but Toad does not. Do you think both Buzzy and Toad work hard to solve their problems?

Before allowing the students to write, the teacher shows them the Thinking Theme Checklist for Comparing Two Texts.

Thinking Theme Checklist for Comparing Two Texts

❑ 1. Do I take a position and clearly answer the question?

❑ 2. Do I support my answer with specific examples and details from both selections?

❑ 3. Do I show how the two reading selections are alike or connected?

❑ 4. Is my response complete?

The teacher reminds students that the first sentence must clearly state a position. The teacher asks them to think about their responses. After thirty seconds of think time, the teacher asks students to show him a thumbs-up if they think Buzzy works hard to solve his problem. All the children respond with a thumbs-up. Next he asks them if they think Toad works hard to solve his problem. After thirty seconds, some children are showing a thumbs-up and others are showing a thumbs-down.

The teacher explains that it is fine for students not to agree as long as they can support their decisions with specific details from the story. Next, he directs their attention to the question and asks them to think how to write the first sentence if they think both Buzzy and Toad work hard to solve their problems and how to write the first sentence if they think Buzzy works hard but Toad does not. The teacher reminds them to think about the words they need from the question and other words they will need to add.

> Buzzy and Toad both have problems to solve. Buzzy solves his problem, but Toad does not. Do you think both Buzzy and Toad work hard to solve their problems?

After thirty seconds of think time, he asks them to turn to their talking partners and discuss what their first sentences will be. Several children share their ideas, and the teacher writes these two possible first sentences on the board:

> I think Buzzy and Toad both work hard to solve their problems.
> I think Buzzy works hard to solve his problem, but Toad does not.

Next the teacher has the children review the information recorded in all four columns on both Thinking Theme charts. He reminds the children that they need to include examples from both stories and use the information from all four columns. They also need to show how the two characters are alike or different in their problem-solving abilities.

The children are given twenty minutes to write their responses. The teacher circulates, giving individual help to students who are struggling. When the time is up, the teacher gathers the children together and chooses a child who has written a good response to read it to the class. The children are asked to listen and see if the writer has done all four things on the checklist and to think of ways to help the writer if something cannot be given a check. The first child (a strong writer!) reads this paragraph:

> I think Buzzy and Toad both work hard to solve their problems. Buzzy needs to get home and he thinks he can't fly. He asks the dragonflies to help. They won't help, but he is smart to ask. He figures out how to climb down from the flower, and he makes a boat to cross the stream. When he gets home, he listens to his parents

and believes them when they tell him he can fly. Toad also works hard to solve his problem. He asks Frog not to look at him. He asks Frog to tell the other animals to go home so they won't see his bathing suit. He stays in the water so they won't see. Finally, he has to come out because he is so cold, and they see his bathing suit. Toad doesn't solve his problem, but he tries hard to solve it.

After this child reads, the teacher leads the children to think about the items on the checklist. The students all agree that the writing does all four things and should get four checks.

Next the teacher asks a child who thought that Toad did not try hard to read her piece. After hearing it, the children decide that even though the two writers disagree, they both clearly state their position, support it with details from both stories, tell how Toad and Buzzy are different, and provide complete answers.

Finally, the teacher asks one more student if he will read his piece. The teacher has already alerted the child that his piece does not have many details to support Buzzy and agrees with the student that it will help everyone write better responses if the class notices this and gives the writer suggestions of details to add. (Note that you have to be careful when asking children to share writing that is less than perfect. But if you choose a confident child and conspire with him or her about how doing this will help everyone, this nonexample can provide a good learning tool. If you are uncomfortable using a less-than-perfect example from one of your students, write one yourself and use it as your nonexample.) This child reads this paragaraph:

I think Buzzy works hard to solve his problem, but Toad does not. Toad just asks people not to look at his bathing suit. Then he just waits in the water. He could have Frog bring him a towel or maybe find another way out. He just asks and waits and doesn't try very hard. Buzzy is a good problem solver, but Toad is not.

After the child reads this piece, the class decides that he gets a check for clearly stating the position and telling how Buzzy and Toad are different, but he needs more examples of how Buzzy works hard. By looking at the Thinking Theme Chart, the other students suggest several details the writer can add that will support that. With these revisions, they feel the writing will be complete and worthy of four checks.

Next the teacher has the children meet in groups of three or four. Each student shares his or her writing, and the group indicates what checks they think each piece should have and what the writer should do to get all the checks. The teacher meets with the group that includes the most-struggling writers in the class.

Writing an extended response connecting characters and theme is a complex and difficult task. Students can learn how to accomplish this, however, if the various parts of the task are taught gradually and supported by modeling and constructive feedback at every step.

To Teach Children How to Write Responses Linking Characters and Theme

1. Teach students to write a clear personal choice statement on a topic of interest.
2. Teach them to write a paragraph, expanding the initial statement by listing reasons for their choice.
3. Teach them to use a checklist to evaluate their personal choice response.

Checklist for Personal Choice Response

1. Do I take a position and clearly answer the question?
2. Do I support my answer with specific examples and details?
3. Is my response complete?

4. Help them transfer their knowledge of how to write a personal choice response to writing a response that links character and theme.
5. Have them evaluate their response using the Thinking Theme Checklist for One Text.

Thinking Theme Checklist for One Text

1. Do I take a position and clearly answer the question?
2. Do I include my definition of the theme?
3. Do I support my answer with specific examples and details from the selection?
4. Is my response complete?

6. Help them transfer their skills to writing a response comparing two texts, and have them evaluate that response using the Thinking Theme Checklist for Comparing Two Texts.

Thinking Theme Checklist for Comparing Two Texts

1. Do I take a position and clearly answer the question?
2. Do I support my answer with specific examples and details from both selections?
3. Do I show how the two reading selections are alike or connected?
4. Is my response complete?

A Sample Lesson Comparing Theme across Two Selections

Photo 1
(p. 87)

nce children begin to understand the concept of theme and how authors show themes by characters' actions, we help them learn to compare themes across two selections. This class of students has been doing Thinking Theme lessons throughout the year, so they know and understand the terms and the procedures. For this lesson, the students are going to read *Teammates,* by Peter Golenbock, and *The Butterfly,* by Patricia Polacco, while thinking about courage. The teacher begins the lesson by displaying the now-familiar Concept Chart and writing *Courage* in the center. She reads the dictionary definition of *courage* to students but reminds them that the definition they write in the definition circle will be one they create using their own words. She then shares with students three scenarios she has planned to help them think about courage.

Scenario 1

There is a class play at school. The teacher says that everyone is going to have a part. You do not want to have any part in the play, because you are afraid to speak in front of a group of people. But the other kids will tease you if you give in to your fear. Will you have the courage to be in the play and speak in front of other people? Are you brave enough to tell the teacher that you are afraid to talk in front of the class?

Scenario 2

You are an orchestra student and really like playing the cello. However, some of your friends think playing the cello is dumb and have started to call you mean names. It's really starting to bother you. You are considering quitting orchestra. Should you quit orchestra to be cool for your friends, or should you have the courage to continue playing the instrument you love?

Scenario 3

Many teachers reward their students for good behavior with special treats. One of your friends sneaks the treat bag one day when you have a substitute teacher and passes out candy to the students. Everyone else is eating the treats and acting like it is no big deal. You are worried that your teacher will be really mad when she comes back tomorrow! What should you do? Do you have the courage not to accept the candy? What is the worst thing that can happen?

After hearing each scenario, the students turn to their talking partners and discuss what they think that scenario tells about courage. Here is one talking partner discussion:

Brandon: I think that courage is obeying the rules even when no one is looking. My mom is always saying that I have to have courage to live the right way even when she is not there.

Elizabeth: What about trying to be brave when you are with your friends?

Brandon: I think we still have courage in our brains even when we don't always act on it. After all, we are just kids!

Shelby: Courage has to do with how we act, not just our beliefs. If we lie about our actions to our friends, then we are not courageous. For example, if the friend makes an excuse like "I don't like chocolate," then he is not brave. If he says that eating the treats is wrong, then he is brave.

Brandon: You can do the right thing by not eating the treats and not making your friends mad, so he is showing courage.

A Sample Lesson Comparing Theme across Two Selections

Elizabeth: If courage is being afraid but still being brave, then the kid who did not eat the candy probably has courage because every kid who did not go along would have courage in spite of the fear.

Photo 2 (p. 87)

Photo 3 (p. 87)

Next the teacher puts the children into groups of three or four and asks them to discuss their own experiences with courage. They try to come up with both examples and nonexamples from their own life experiences.

After this small-group discussion, the class gathers together and fills in information on the Concept Chart for Courage based on their own experiences. Here's part of the class discussion:

Antonio: One time last year, I was brave when I told my friend not to pick on another kid on the playground. I was afraid my friend would get mad at me. I think that is courage.

Alison: I was afraid to stay home alone. That is not courage.

Amy: I think that I had a lot of courage when I played my flute in my recital, even though I was really scared to play in front of people.

Concept Chart for Courage

Examples (from own life)	Nonexamples (from own life)
Told my friend not to bully a little kid Played in a piano recital even though I was afraid Stayed home alone in the dark Riding roller coasters even though I'm afraid	Refused to stay alone Gave in to peer pressure Called someone a wimp for not doing what everyone else was doing
Example characteristics	**Nonexample characteristics**
Doing what is right even if you are worried Trying something for the first time Doing something to save someone, risking your life Telling others to stop picking on someone Doing something daring	Running away from a problem Running away from trouble Not standing up for what you believe Being scared to try something Being afraid to help
Examples from books	**Nonexamples from books**

Definition:

Courage —
to keep going and be brave even when you are afraid

Next the teacher shows the students what they will read today, *Teammates,* by Peter Golenbock.

Summary of *Teammates*

Teammates is the story of two famous baseball players—one white and one black—who play together on the same Major League Baseball team, breaking the color barrier that existed in professional sports in the United States. In spite of the culture of segregation and prejudice in the United States at the time, these men find the strength within themselves to accept and respect each other both as players and as men.

The teacher introduces some key vocabulary concepts for *Teammates* by drawing two concept circles on the board and leading a class discussion. In the first concept circle, she fills in three of the four boxes by writing *Civil rights movement*, *Keeping apart by law,* and *Blacks away from whites.* The teacher asks the students to think about what one word these words and phrases are describing. How are these words related to each other? She asks them to take thirty seconds to talk with their partners about what word should go in the fourth box.

Blacks away from whites | Civil rights movement

Keeping apart by law | ?

As the partners talk, she can see by the looks on their faces that several (but not all) have come up with the word *segregation.* She lets the ones who have figured this out explain how they decided the word was *segregation.* Then she writes it in the fourth box.

A Sample Lesson Comparing Theme across Two Selections

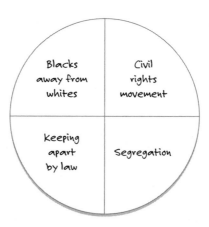

The teacher then introduces the second concept circle with these words and phrases: *Brave, Willing to try something new,* and *Confidence to try when afraid.* The talking partners quickly begin to talk, and this time most of them come up with the word *courage.* They look quite proud of themselves as the teacher completes the concept circle with the word *Courage.*

Next the teacher displays the Thinking Theme Chart students are going to complete after reading *Teammates.* They read the big question and review the familiar questions in the four columns. Because they have been doing Thinking Theme Charts all year, all the students understand that their job while reading today will be to find a character's actions that they think connect to the theme. They also understand that they need to think about

Photo 4 (p. 88)

why the character acts this way, what the character **gets** for acting this way, and if this event shows the **theme** of courage?

Thinking Theme Chart for Courage

Big Question:			
Which characters in <u>Teammates</u> do you think show courage, and how do they show it?			
Event or **actions** by characters connected to the theme, including examples and nonexamples	**Why** does the character act this way?	What does the character **get** for acting this way?	Does this event show the **theme** of courage? Yes, because *or* No, because

The teacher hands one book to each set of reading partners and asks them to find the first sticky flag. She then explains that, as she often does, she will help students get into the book by reading aloud to them up to the first sticky flag. She asks them to follow along in the book as she reads and to think about events they want to add to the Thinking Theme Chart. The teacher does not let children interrupt her while she is reading, but she can tell by watching their eyes look up at the Thinking Theme Chart that they are thinking about the events and what they mean.

When the teacher gets to the first sticky flag, she gives students two minutes to talk with their partners about what they think should be added to the chart. When the two minutes is up, children are all eager to share ideas. They discuss the events and agree on two they want added to the chart. The teacher writes these two events and then leads students to think about why each event happens, what the character gets out of the event, and if the event is an example of courage. For each column, she listens to all the students' responses and then records the things they agree on before moving to the next question.

Stop and think!

Photo 5 (p. 88)

Thinking Theme Chart for Couarge: After Read-Along

Big Question: Which characters in <u>Teammates</u> do you think show courage, and how do they show it?			
Event or **actions** by characters connected to the theme, including examples and nonexamples	**Why** does the character act this way?	What does the character **get** for acting this way?	Does this event show the **theme** of courage? Yes, because *or* No, because
Branch Rickey decides to give everyone a chance to play baseball, regardless of his or her color.	He wants to win the game. He believes everyone deserves to play, regardless of race.	He has a chance to win, a chance to meet the best players, and a chance to change people's minds.	Yes, because other people judged him.
Branch Rickey launches a search for the best player with self-control.	He wants to win the game. He believes everyone deserves to play, regardless of race.	He has a chance to win, a chance to meet the best players, and a chance to meet the best black players.	Yes, because other people judged him.

Stop and think!

The teacher then points out the sticky flags she has placed at the bottoms of several pages in the book and reminds students that when they reach a page with a sticky flag, they should stop and discuss the character's actions to that point and reflect on the Thinking Theme Chart. These students understand that stopping at the sticky flag allows them to chunk the selection and have time to reflect and discuss. The teacher tells the students that they will be reading with their reading partners today and that she will be coming around to coach them as they read. Before sending the children off to finish the story, she asks,

"What is your job as you are reading today?"

The children quickly respond that their job is to find events that tell something about the characters and the theme and to be ready to share those events and complete the Thinking Theme Chart.

Photo 6 (p. 88)

The children smoothly move to their quiet spots in the room to read with their partners. They begin reading, and the teacher can tell by the way their eyes look at the Concept Chart for Courage and the Thinking Theme Chart that they are thinking about what the characters do and what that tells them about the theme. The teacher circulates, spending a minute or two with four or five partnerships and coaching them in their reading and thinking. As she interacts with one set of partners, she realizes that they do not need help reading the text or interacting with each other, but they do need help having a deeper conversation about theme. They seem to need help moving beyond saying "This is about courage!" She asks,

> "Do you think that Pee Wee wants to lose his job, or does he have confidence in his ability, which gives him courage? Why does he have courage?"

These questions help the partners focus on theme. Mary answers that Pee Wee wants to play baseball. He also believes that everyone is allowed to play baseball. "That is courage," she says. The teacher moves to another partner group.

After fourteen minutes, the children gather together and pool their thoughts to complete the chart. The teacher pushes the students to think deeply about the events they want to list. In the **Events** column, she writes,

> Pee Wee puts his arm around his teammate Jackie, declaring they are teammates.

Then the teacher asks students **why** they think Pee Wee did that. She accepts several answers, including the following:

> "He has integrity."
> "It's the right thing to do."
> "He knew it was time to show fans that Jackie is his teammate."

The teacher asks students for the next key word. They answer "Get." The teacher acknowledges their correct response and expands on it, asking what Pee Wee **gets** for acting this way. Students give these answers:

> "Respect of Jackie."
> "Eventually respect of the world."

The teacher points to the next column and the key word **theme.** She explains that the last step is thinking about what characters do and how to connect to the theme. She tells students,

> "Our theme today is courage. Does Pee Wee's putting his arm around Jackie tell us anything about courage? Show me a thumbs-up if you think this event tells us something about courage."

A Sample Lesson Comparing Theme across Two Selections

All the students signal a thumbs-up, and the teacher calls on one student to explain how this event shows courage. The student explains:

> "Yes, this is courage because all the fans could have turned on Pee Wee, so Pee Wee had to be really brave to put his arm around his black teammate."

Here is the Thinking Theme Chart at the end of the lesson.

Thinking Theme Chart for Courage: Completed

Big Question:			
Which characters in <u>Teammates</u> do you think show courage, and how do they show it?			
Event or **actions** by characters connected to the theme, including examples and nonexamples	**Why** does the character act this way?	What does the character **get** for acting this way?	Does this event show the **theme** of courage? Yes, because or No, because
Branch Rickey decides to give everyone a chance to play baseball, regardless of his or her color.	He wants to win the game. He believes everyone deserves to play, regardless of race.	He has a chance to win, a chance to meet the best players, and a chance to change people's minds.	Yes, because other people judged him.
Branch Rickey launches a search for the best player with self-control.	He wants to win the game. He believes everyone deserves to play, regardless of race.	He has a chance to win, a chance to meet the best players, and a chance to meet the best black players.	Yes, because other people judged him.
Jackie Robinson agrees not to fight back, to have self-control.	He wants to play Major League Baseball.	He gets baseball-playing time and to be part of "the great experiment."	Yes, because he is brave to be the first and only black player.
Players avoid Jackie and are even mean to him.	They are men from South and are afraid of him.	They get to ignore the situation and pretend Jackie will go away.	No, this is not courage. This is being nasty and mean!

Jackie doesn't give up even though the baseball players are mean.	He really wants to be a baseball player. He doesn't want to give up his dream. He doesn't want to disappoint his parents and Branch Rickey.	He makes the Brooklyn Dodgers Major League Baseball team!	Yes, because not giving up when no one is nice is hard! It would be easier to give up.
Pee Wee says that Jackie can have his job if he is better.	He has integrity.	?	Yes, it takes courage to risk your job to do the right thing.
Pee Wee won't sign the petition that his teammates circulate.	He believes Jackie has the right to play. He doesn't care what color Jackie is.	He gets teased. People avoid and roll their eyes at him.	Yes, it takes courage to stand up to your teammates and say no.
Fans yell hateful things at Jackie.	They don't think Jackie has the right to play Major League Baseball.	They have angry, mean feelings.	No, because the fans form a mob
Jackie holds in his anger.	He wants to keep playing. He doesn't want to give them an excuse to fire him.	He gets to keep playing.	Yes, it is still courage to hold onto your temper.
Pee Wee puts his arm around his teammate Jackie, declaring they are teammates.	He has integrity; it is right thing to do. He knows it's time to show fans that Jackie is his teammate.	He gets the respect of Jackie and eventually the respect of the world.	Yes, because all the fans could have turned on Pee Wee.

The teacher says,

"Now that we have read *Teammates* and thought about courage in this book, let's see what examples and nonexamples we can add to our Concept Chart."

The students feel there are many examples of courage in *Teammates*. The teacher leads them to decide on the clearest, most memorable examples of courage, and they add these to the chart.

Concept Chart for Courage: Completed

Examples (from own life)		Nonexamples (from own life)
Told my friend not to bully a little kid Played in a piano recital even though I was afraid Stayed home alone in the dark Riding roller coasters even though I'm afraid	**Definition:** Courage — to keep going and be brave even when you are afraid	Refused to stay alone Gave in to peer pressure Called someone a wimp for not doing what everyone else was doing
Example characteristics Doing what is right even if you are worried Trying something for the first time Doing something to save someone, risking your life Telling others to stop picking on someone Doing something daring		**Nonexample characteristics** Running away from a problem Running away from trouble Not standing up for what you believe Being scared to try something Being afraid to help
Examples from books Teammates Jackie holds in his anger and doesn't give up. Pee Wee refuses to sign the petition and puts his arm around Jackie. Branch Rickey gives Jackie a chance.		**Nonexamples from books** Teammates Fans yell mean things at Jackie. Players refuse to eat with Jackie.

The next selection the teacher has chosen to have the students think about courage is *The Butterfly,* by Patricia Polacco. This is a longer and more complex story, and the teacher knows her students will need a lot of knowledge building to make sense of it. To begin building background knowledge about the Holocaust, the teacher had read aloud *The Lily Cupboard* to her students. Before introducing *The Butterfly,* the teacher reminds them of *The Lily Cupboard.* She lists some of the words from *The Lily Cupboard* that are also important in *The Butterfly* and has students use them to summarize what happened in *The Lily Cupboard* and what they know about the Holocaust:

occupation	hid	Nazis
Jews	war	soldiers
Holocaust		

Next, the teacher introduces *The Butterfly* and tells students that this story is also about courage.

Summary of *The Butterfly*—Part 1, pages 1–11

The Butterfly takes place in Nazi-occupied France in the 1940s. In a small country village, several citizens work with the resistance movement to hide Jews from Nazi soldiers. In one family, the mother has been keeping a secret from her family. She has been sheltering, hiding, and protecting Jews without the rest of the family's knowledge. Over several days, the mother's secret is discovered by her daughter.

Because there are a lot of characters and vocabulary to introduce, the teacher begins the lesson by reading aloud to her students the first third of the story. She doesn't direct them to the Thinking Theme Chart yet but asks them just to listen for who the characters are and what they are doing in the story. She lists these characters on the board and has the children pronounce the names with her:

Monique

Pinouff

Ghost child

Madame Marcel Solliliage

Denise

Monsieur Marks

Nazi soldiers

Pere Voulliard

Sevrine

When the teacher has finished reading aloud the selection she has chosen, she and the children name each of the characters and discuss what has happened in the story so far. As they talk about the characters and events, the teacher makes sure to include other difficult but important vocabulary, including *France, the war, the occupation, Jews,* and *Nazis.*

After reading and summarizing the first third of the book, the teacher draws the children's attention to the Thinking Theme Chart and has them read the big question:

Photo 7 (p. 89)

Photo 8 (p. 89)

Which characters in *The Butterfly* do you think show courage, and how do they show it?

The children immediately recognize that the big question is exactly the same one they thought about as they read *Teammates*. The teacher them tells them that they are going to read with their reading partners the same pages she just read to them and think about events they want to add to the chart. She hands each partnership one book, and the children notice that she has placed three sticky flags at places where she wants them to stop and talk.

Stop and think!

Thinking Theme Chart for *Courage*

Big Question: Which characters in <u>The Butterfly</u> do you think show courage, and how do they show it?			
Event or **actions** by characters connected to the theme, including examples and nonexamples	**Why** does the character act this way?	What does the character **get** for acting this way?	Does this event show the **theme** of courage? Yes, because *or* No, because

Photo 9
(p. 89)

The partners read and talk together for sixteen minutes. As they read, the teacher circulates and coaches the children in their reading and thinking. When the time is up, the teacher gathers the students together and directs their attention to the chart. The children discuss events they think say something about a character's courage, and the teacher re-cords these events on the chart. For each event, the teacher asks students why they think the character does it, what the character gets out of doing it, and whether this action shows courage. Here is the Thinking Theme Chart at the end of day 1.

Thinking Theme Chart for Courage: Day 1

Big Question: Which characters in <u>The Butterfly</u> do you think show courage, and how do they show it?			
Event or **actions** by characters connected to the theme, including examples and nonexamples	**Why** does the character act this way?	What does the character **get** for acting this way?	Does this event show the **theme** of courage? Yes, because *or* No, because
Monique finds the ghost girl sitting on her bed.	Monique just wakes up.	Monique is curious and even wonders if it was a dream.	No, Monique is not really showing courage. Yes, it takes courage to talk to a ghost.
The ghost girl runs away.	She is scared.	She gets out of the room and doesn't get caught.	No, the ghost girl is not showing courage because she ran.

The Nazi soldiers take Monsieur Marks away.	They are rounding up Jews and taking them away.	This is their job.	No, the soldiers are not brave. They have guns and there are lots of them.
Monique and Denise want to run away but they don't.	They are afraid that if they run, they will be taken away, too.	They are safe and run home.	Yes, because it takes courage to talk and laugh and not run away.
Monique sees the ghost child holding Pinouff and keeps her from running away.	Monique knows it wasn't a dream because Pinouff was purring. She wants to know who the girl is.	Monique finds out the girl's name is Sevrine and that Sevrine lives in Monique's house.	Yes, it takes courage to talk to Sevrine and stop her from running away.

On the following day, the teacher and children review the events they have recorded from the first third of *The Butterfly*. The teacher tells them they are going to use a three-ring circus format to read the next part of the story. She shows them the chart, and the children understand how they will read it.

Photo 10 (p. 90)

She tells the children that they will have twenty minutes to read today and reminds them that they need to be ready to add events and reasons to the chart. She makes sure that the students know what to do if they finish before the timer sounds:

"If you finish before the timer dings, write down the one event you think shows something about courage and why the character does it, what the character gets from doing it, and if the character is showing courage when he or she does this."

Photo 11 (p. 90)

Three-Ring Circus Format

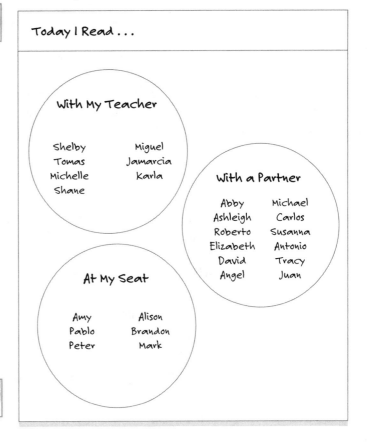

Today I Read . . .

With My Teacher

Shelby   Miguel
Tomas   Jamarcia
Michelle   Karla
Shane

With a Partner

Abby   Michael
Ashleigh   Carlos
Roberto   Susanna
Elizabeth   Antonio
David   Tracy
Angel   Juan

At My Seat

Amy   Alison
Pablo   Brandon
Peter   Mark

A Sample Lesson Comparing Theme across Two Selections

Summary of *The Butterfly*—Part 2, pages 12–23

The young girl has discovered the secret that her mother and other villagers have kept for a long time: They have been hiding Jewish families from the Nazis. After coming in contact with the daughter of the Jewish family hiding in her cellar, the two girls become friends and try to create as normal a friendship as possible. All goes well until one fateful night, when the girls get a little careless.

The children quickly get into their reading. The group meeting with the teacher includes four struggling readers and two average readers. She asks them to read to the first sticky flag. As they read, she coaches the two readers sitting on either side of her as they decode the text. Two of the children get to the first sticky flag ahead of the other four, and the teacher directs their attention to the questions on the chart. When everyone arrives at the first sticky flag, the teacher leads them to talk about what events show courage, why the character does this, what he or she gets out of it, and what this says about courage. They continue reading, stopping at the flags for the teacher-led discussion until the timer sounds.

When the timer sounds, the group reading with the teacher has not yet gotten to the last sticky flag. The teacher assures them that they shouldn't worry about finishing and that they will learn what happened in the part they haven't read from the discussion that accompanies the completion of the chart. The teacher knows that this group often will not complete the text. In these coaching groups, the teacher always concentrates on the quality of the thinking she can get the students reading with her to do. She doesn't worry about how much text gets read.

The class assembles by the Thinking Theme Chart, and everyone is eager to suggest events. Again the teacher pushes them to think about **why** events happened, what the characters **got** from the events, and if the events were examples or nonexamples of the **theme** of courage. Here is some of the discussion that went on:

> **Miguel:** Let's discuss the event. Madame Solliliage? She knows! They aren't the only ones that she had helped.
>
> **Alison:** We have to answer *why*.
>
> **Miguel:** I don't know the why, but I know she has courage because the Nazis could kill her if she is caught.
>
> **Pablo:** I think the *why* is Mrs. Solliliage has guts to help even though she could die.
>
> **Alison:** What does Madame Solliliage get then? Dead?!
>
> **Pablo [chuckling]:** NO! She is really brave.

Allison: I don't think so. I think she is risking her family. They could get killed.

Miguel: It is definitely courage though. It is brave to chance dying.

The teacher closes the lesson by leading a discussion about courage. She asks the students what types of courage the characters exhibit in the story. Have students experienced any courage in their own lives today? The students sigh with compliance that the lesson is over, and they have to wait another day for the ending.

Photo 13 (p. 91)

Here is the Thinking Theme Chart at the end of day 2.

Thinking Theme Chart for Courage: Day 2

Big Question:
Which characters in <u>The Butterfly</u> do you think show courage, and how do they show it?

Event or actions by characters connected to the theme, including examples and nonexamples	Why does the character act this way?	What does the character get for acting this way?	Does this event show the theme of courage? Yes, because or No, because
Monique finds the ghost girl sitting on her bed.	Monique just wakes up.	Monique is curious and even wonders if it was a dream.	No, Monique is not really showing courage. Yes, it takes courage to talk to a ghost.
The ghost girl runs away.	She is scared.	She gets out of the room and doesn't get caught.	No, the ghost girl is not showing courage because she ran.
The Nazi soldiers take Monsieur Marks away.	They are rounding up Jews and taking them away.	This is their job.	No, the soldiers are not brave. They have guns and there are lots of them.
Monique and Denise want to run away but they don't.	They are afraid that if they run, they will be taken away, too.	They are safe and run home.	Yes, because it takes courage to talk and laugh and not run away.
Monique sees the ghost child holding Pinouff and keeps her from running away.	Monique knows it wasn't a dream because Pinouff was purring. She wants to know who the girl is.	Monique finds out the girl's name is Sevrine and that Sevrine lives in Monique's house.	Yes, it takes courage to talk to Sevrine and stop her from running away.
Sevrine shows Monique the hidden room in the cellar.	Sevrine has to explain how she can be in the house.	Sevrine gets a friend even though she is in hiding.	Yes, Sevrine is courageous because she trusts Monique will keep her secret.

continued

A Sample Lesson Comparing Theme across Two Selections

The soldier kills the butterfly.	He is just showing off and being mean.	??	No, it doesn't take any courage to kill a butterfly.
Monique and Sevrine play together in Monique's room late at night.	They want to be friends. They are trying to have a normal life.	They get to pretend that there is no danger and that it is OK to just be kids.	Yes, they are both courageous because they are taking chances and risk being caught, but being friends is more important.
Monique and Sevrine are seen by a neighbor and tell Madame Solliliage.	The girls are playing and don't realize that they have drawn attention to themselves.	They get nervous and worried.	Yes, both girls show courage because even though they are scared, they tell Madame Solliliage.

Summary of *The Butterfly*—Part 3, pages 24–37

The worst has happened. During one of their nightly celebrations of friendship, the girls become careless and are seen by a neighbor. Knowing both families are in danger, plans are made to move the hiding Jewish family to a new safe house. While trying to keep both families safe, each girl becomes separated from her parents. One family is able to reunite safely, while the safety of the other is in doubt. A single butterfly offers hope that both families have been reunited and are safe.

Stop and think!

Photo 14 (p. 91)

On the third day, the students are excited to read the ending of *The Butterfly*. The teacher tells the students that they will finish the story by reading in teams today. She has appointed a coach for each group. These children have read in teams before, and they all like reading this way—particularly when they get their turn to be the coach. The teacher gives the books to the coaches of the groups and huddles with them for a minute, making sure that they know how to stop everyone at the sticky flags and discuss events they think should be added to the chart.

The coaches take their groups to different places in the room, and the children are all eager to begin reading and see how *The Butterfly* ends. The teacher circulates, spending a minute or two with each team and coaching them in their reading and thinking. After twenty minutes, the class comes together to complete the Thinking Theme Chart.

Thinking Theme for Courage: Day 3

Big Question:

Which characters in <u>The Butterfly</u> do you think show courage, and how do they show it?

Event or **actions** by characters connected to the theme, including examples and nonexamples	**Why** does the character act this way?	What does the character **get** for acting this way?	Does this event show the **theme** of courage? Yes, because or No, because
Monique finds the ghost girl sitting on her bed.	Monique just wakes up.	Monique is curious and even wonders if it was a dream.	No, Monique is not really showing courage. Yes, it takes courage to talk to a ghost.
The ghost girl runs away.	She is scared.	She gets out of the room and doesn't get caught.	No, the ghost girl is not showing courage because she ran.
The Nazi soldiers take Monsieur Marks away.	They are rounding up Jews and taking them away.	This is their job.	No, the soldiers are not brave. They have guns and there are lots of them.
Monique and Denise want to run away but they don't.	They are afraid that if they run, they will be taken away, too.	They are safe and run home.	Yes, because it takes courage to talk and laugh and not run away.
Monique sees the ghost child holding Pinouff and keeps her from running away.	Monique knows it wasn't a dream because Pinouff was purring. She wants to know who the girl is.	Monique finds out the girl's name is Sevrine and that Sevrine lives in Monique's house.	Yes, it takes courage to talk to Sevrine and stop her from running away.
Sevrine shows Monique the hidden room in the cellar.	Sevrine has to explain how she can be in the house.	Sevrine gets a friend even though she is in hiding.	Yes, Sevrine is courageous because she trusts Monique will keep her secret.
The soldier kills the butterfly.	He is just showing off and being mean.	??	No, it doesn't take any courage to kill a butterfly.
Monique and Sevrine play together in Monique's room late at night.	They want to be friends. They are trying to have a normal life.	They get to pretend that there is no danger and that it is OK to just be kids.	Yes, they are both courageous because they are taking chances and risk being caught, but being friends is more important.

continued

A Sample Lesson Comparing Theme across Two Selections

Monique and Sevrine are seen by a neighbor and tell Madame Solliliage.	The girls are playing and don't realize that they have drawn attention to themselves.	They get nervous and worried.	Yes, both girls show courage because even though they are scared, they tell Madame Solliliage.
Madame Solliliage arranges for the family to leave.	Madame knows the family is no longer safe hiding in her house.	??	Yes, Madame shows courage by not giving in to her fears. She is trying to protect both families.
Madame, Monique, and Sevrine walk all night.	They are taking Sevrine to meet her parents.	Sevrine will be safe.	Yes, they are all courageous. They almost get caught by a Nazi patrol car.
Monique and her mother get separated at the train station.	They didn't plan it. They are separated by the crowd of people trying to get through the gate.	Both feel scared. Monique is crying. She tries to be brave and get home alone.	Yes, because Monique gets home by herself.

The next step in this Thinking Theme lesson is to add ideas from *The Butterfly* to the Concept Chart. Since there are so many events in *The Butterfly,* the teacher leads the children in deciding which events are the best examples and then adds these to the chart (see next page).

The next day, the teacher tells students they have done their jobs very well and have done excellent thinking about courage the last four days. Then she writes the following writing prompt on the board:

> There are many examples of courage in both *Teammates* and *The Butterfly.* Pick two characters—one from *Teammates* and one from *The Butterfly*—who you think should be awarded a medal of courage. Defend your choice by using specific details and examples from both selections.

Before the students start writing, the teacher gives them four minutes to talk with their partners about which characters they will choose and which events they will use to support their opinions. Partners Roberto and Susanna begin talking immediately about which characters they will choose. Roberto is sure that Jackie Robinson shows the most courage in *Teammates,* and Susanna agrees. They do not agree, however, on who shows the most courage in *The Butterfly.* Roberto thinks it is Marcel because she hides the family in the house and arranges for them to escape. Susanna agrees that Marcel shows courage, but she thinks Monique is even more courageous—considering she is just a kid. Susanna explains,

"Monique is brave all through the story. She is brave when she doesn't let Sevrine run away and when she doesn't run away when the Nazis take Monsieur Marks. She is really brave when she tells her mother she thinks a neighbor has seen her and Sevrine and when she walks home by herself."

When the four minutes of talking time is up, all the children quickly take out their reading-response notebooks and begin to write. The eyes of all the children can be seen glancing up at the Thinking Theme Charts for both *Teammates* and *The Butterfly* and the

Concept Chart for Courage: Complete

Examples (from own life)		Nonexamples (from own life)
Told my friend not to bully a little kid Played in a piano recital even though I was afraid Stayed home alone in the dark Riding roller coasters even though I'm afraid	**Definition:** Courage — to keep going and be brave even when you are afraid	Refused to stay alone Gave in to peer pressure Called someone a wimp for not doing what everyone else was doing
Example characteristics		**Nonexample characteristics**
Doing what is right even if you are worried Trying something for the first time Doing something to save someone, risking your life Telling others to stop picking on someone Doing something daring		Running away from a problem Running away from trouble Not standing up for what you believe believe Being scared to try something Being afraid to help
Examples from books		**Nonexamples from books**
Examples from Teammates Jackie holds in his anger and doesn't give up. Pee Wee refuses to sign the petition and puts his arm around Jackie. Branch Rickey gives Jackie a chance. Examples from The Butterfly Marcel hides Jews from the Nazis. The girls tell the mother when they are seen by the neighbor. Monique gets home by herself.		Nonexamples from Teammates Fans yell mean things at Jackie. Players refuse to eat with Jackie. Nonexamples from The Butterfly The soldier kills the butterfly.

Concept Chart for Courage. As the children write, the teacher circulates, stopping to coach those who need some extra support to complete this complex task.

When the writing time is up, the teacher gathers the students, and volunteers read or tell what they have written. Not everyone agrees on which characters should get a medal of courage, but all the students have chosen good examples from the texts to back up their choices. To complete the lesson, the children use the Thinking Theme Checklist to evaluate their responses.

Thinking Theme Checklist for Comparing Two Texts

❑ 1. Do I take a position and clearly answer the question?

❑ 2. Do I support my answer with specific examples and details from both selections?

❑ 3. Do I show how the two reading selections are alike or connected?

❑ 4. Is my response complete?

Teaching a Thinking Theme Lesson Connecting Two Texts

1. Choose two stories with the same theme. Be sure each story contains several events that are examples or nonexamples of the theme.

2. Compose a big question that connects the characters in both stories with the theme.

3. Along with your students, create a Concept Chart for the theme based on personal experiences you share with them and their own personal experiences with the theme.

4. Introduce the first story to the class along with the big question they will need to do deep thinking about.

5. Introduce character names and other key vocabulary for the first story.

6. Show children the Thinking Theme Chart they will complete after reading the first story.

7. Have children read all or part of the story, stopping at the sticky flags to reflect on the characters' actions and the theme.

8. Complete the Thinking Theme Chart together for the first story

9. Repeat steps 4–8 for the second story.

10. Complete the Concept Chart by adding examples and nonexamples from both stories.

11. Have children write their answers to the big question, backing up their opinions with facts and details from both stories.

12. Have children evaluate their response using the Thinking Theme Checklist for Comparing Two Texts.

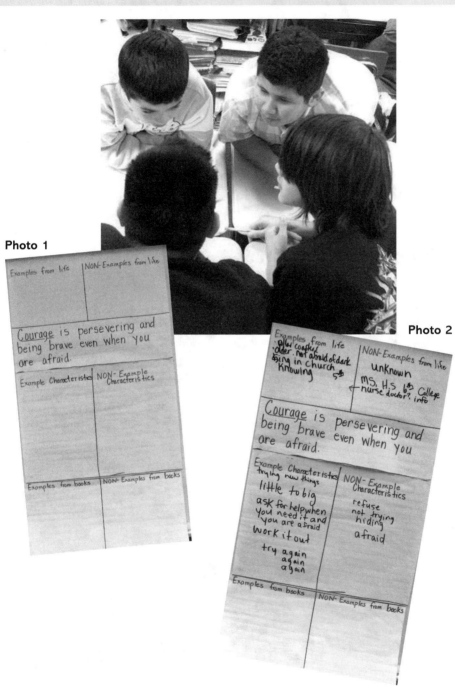

Photo 1

Examples from life | NON-Examples from life

<u>Courage</u> is persevering and being brave even when you are afraid.

Example Characteristics | NON-Example Characteristics

Examples from books | NON-Examples from books

Photo 2

Examples from life
Roller coaster
Older. not afraid of dark
Being in church
Knowing 5th

NON-Examples from life
unknown
MS, H.S 6th College
nurse doctor? info

<u>Courage</u> is persevering and being brave even when you are afraid.

Example Characteristics
trying new things
little to big
ask for help when you need it and you are afraid
work it out
try again
again
again

NON-Example Characteristics
refuse
not trying
hiding
afraid

Examples from books | NON-Examples from books

Photo 3

87

Photo 4

Photo 5

Photo 6

Photo 7

Monique   ghost child

Pinouff (cat)

Madame Marcel Solliliage
  (Mrs)
           Nazi soldiers

Denise

Monsieur Marks
  (Mr.)
           Jews/Jewish

Pere Voulliard
(Father)   Resistence

Sevrine

BIG QUESTION: Which characters in _The Butterfly_ do you think showed courage and how did they show it?

Photo 8

Photo 9

Events ... Actions	Why?	Get?	Connected to the theme ... because ...
The Nazi kills the butterfly.	· He's mean · wants to scare her	· Makes Monique afraid · Makes others afraid	No ... because the soldier is bigger. It's easy for him to be mean.
Monique + Sevrine play together late at night.	· They're kids · Kids like to play	· Friendship · A chance to be normal and happy	Yes ... because they have the courage to be together even though they could get in trouble.
Monique + Sevrine are seen by a neighbor + tell Madame Solliliage	· They forgot · They were careless · They were having fun and forgot	· Worried · Nervous · Trouble	Yes ... the girls know they messed up and now they have to tell the adult — (Madame)

Photo 10

Photo 11

Photo 12

PHOTO GALLERY

Photo 13

Photo 14

Organizing for Thinking Theme Lessons across the Year

Y ou now know almost everything you need to know about teaching Thinking Theme lessons:

- You know how to choose selections with strong themes and probably have several stories in mind that are well suited for theme thinking and that you know your students will enjoy.

- You know how to use the adapted Frayer model chart and build a rich concept of themes based on scenarios you share with your students and their own experiences with the theme.

- You know how to frame the *big question* so that students will do *deep thinking* about the theme, which we often call the *big idea*.

- You know how to set up your Thinking Theme Chart so students will be clear that their purpose for reading is to identify events that link characters with theme.

- You know how to divide the text into reasonable chunks using sticky flags to designate *stop, think, and talk* points and the stopping point for the day's reading.

Stop and think!

- You know how to lead your students to fill in the chart, thinking about each event, why it happens, what the character gets from this event, and what this event shows about the character and the theme.

- You remember that sometimes your students will not agree on why events happen or what they show about the theme and are prepared to record dissenting opinions when your students can back them up.

- You know that sometimes no one will know what goes in a particular column on the chart and have given yourself permission to put several question marks in that box and move on. (Deep thinking is seldom neat and tidy!)

- You know how to construct a writing prompt so that your students will respond to the theme, stating their opinion and backing it up with facts and details from the selection.

- You know how to evaluate—and teach your students to evaluate—their thinking by using a checklist or scale to score their responses.

You are almost ready to add Thinking Theme lessons to your repertoire of comprehension lesson frameworks and dramatically increase the amount of higher-level thinking about text in which your students engage. The remaining issue for you to think about is how you will organize your students for Thinking Theme lessons. In this chapter, we will suggest a framework for Thinking Theme lessons that provides a lot of support early in the year so that you and the students are sure to experience success. As the year goes on, the students will take more responsibility for all aspects of the lessons. By the end of the year, we expect all students to be able to read a text on their level, identify a theme for that text, and independently write a response. If that sounds too good to be true, suspend disbelief as you read this chapter and think about how you will achieve this gradual release of responsibility.

Begin the Year with Teacher Read-Alouds and Familiar Themes

When you and your students are taking on a new task, make everything else about that task as easy as possible. We begin teaching our students to think deeply about themes and characters by choosing a story we know they will enjoy and reading it aloud to them. When students are listening to us read, they do not have to divide their attention between the two tasks of identifying words and thinking. Their only job while listening is thinking—deep thinking about the characters and the theme.

From our standpoint as teachers, planning a Thinking Theme lesson where the text is read aloud makes life easier for us, too! Unlike later lessons, where we have to consider how to get multiple copies of the texts for children to read, for this first lesson, we only need one book. In later lessons, we will need to think about the different reading levels of students in our classroom and how to provide support for students for whom word identification demands make the text too difficult to read on their own. When choosing a text we will read to them, we don't need to worry about the text being too hard for some students. Rather, we can choose a text solely because it has the strong theme we want to begin with and is one both we and the students will love.

In this first lesson, you are going to be teaching students things that will be new to many of them. Many of your students won't really know what a theme is, and they won't have thought much about how authors show themes by what characters do and how they interact. Most elementary students have a very narrow concept of theme and how it plays out in text. So begin with a theme your children are very familiar with and one that is important to them. Most children know more about cooperation and courage than they do about perseverance. They probably know more about perseverance than they do about integrity or respect. The most common theme in children's books and the one they know most about and care most about is probably friendship. So to launch your students on a successful journey of theme thinking, why not begin with the concept of friendship?

There are so many children's books in which friendship is a strong theme that your problem will not be finding one but rather choosing the one or two you and the children will enjoy most. Once you have chosen the text, follow the steps in planning and teaching your lesson. Here are our Thinking Theme lesson steps adapted for a read-aloud lesson early in the year.

The First Thinking Theme Lesson Using a Read-Aloud Text

Choose a Story with a Strong and Familiar Theme

Be sure the story contains several events that illustrate the theme. For this first lesson, it is probably best to choose a short book, which can be read and charted in one day. We are using *The Other Side,* by Jacqueline Woodson, for the first lesson teaching the theme of friendship.

Read the Story Once to Students without Focusing on the Theme

In the first reading, allow students just to think about and enjoy the story. If you have chosen a book they enjoy, they will be delighted when you pull it out on another day and ask them to think with you about the theme.

Compose a Big Question That Connects the Characters with the Theme

Your first big question should be as simple as possible and should let students know that you want their opinion. Here's an example:

> How do you think Clover and Anne show friendship?

Along with Your Students, Create a Concept Chart for the Theme

Seat your students in talking partners, and share three scenarios you have made up about friendship. Give students thirty seconds to talk about each scenario and the theme, and then have volunteers share their thoughts. Next put students in groups of three or four, and give them six minutes to talk about what being a good friend does and does not mean. Then, gather students together and let them share their thoughts and experiences. Record examples and nonexamples, characteristics and noncharacteristics, and a kid-friendly definition on your Concept Chart for Friendship.

Stop and think!

Concept Chart for Friendship

Examples (from own life)	Definition:	Nonexamples (from own life)
Played together nicely Gave someone a pencil Sat with the new kid at lunch Asked someone his name	Friendship — when friends spend time together, show kindness to each other, and are loyal to each other	Stuck out tongue Ignored someone Not sharing stuff Saying "You cannot play!"
Example characteristics Getting along with people Sharing with everyone Taking turns at home and school		**Nonexample characteristics** Fighting and disagreeing Kicking, being mean, pushing Calling names and being rude Ignoring others
Examples from books		**Nonexamples from books**

Show Students the Big Question about Which They Will Do Deep Thinking

Show students the book you have chosen to focus this first lesson on, and explain that you are going to read it again to them. But this time, they have a very important job. Their job is to think about the big question.

> How do you think Clover and Anne show friendship?

Show Students the Thinking Theme Chart They Will Help You Complete

Talk about each column in the chart, and help children understand what they need to think about to answer the questions in each column.

> "In the first column, we are going to list some events in the story that show us something about what good friends Anne and Clover are to each other. In the next column, we are going to do some deep thinking about why the girls do this. In the third column, we are going to try to figure out what the girls get out of doing this. In the last column, we are going to put what we think this shows about the theme—how the girls are good friends to each other."

Thinking Theme Chart for Friendship

Big Question:			
How do you think Clover and Anne show friendship?			
Event or **actions** by characters connected to the theme, including examples and nonexamples	**Why** does the character act this way?	What does the character **get** for acting this way?	Does this event show the **theme** of friendship? Yes, because *or* No, because

Seat your children in talking partners. Read the story aloud to them, stopping at the sticky flags you have placed at strategic points and having the children talk about the characters' actions and the theme. Show your students the sticky flags, and explain that you have marked these places because they are good points to stop and talk about things the characters have done. When you get to a sticky flag, point to your chart and ask this question:

"What do Clover and Anne do here?"

After the children tell you what happened, record the event in the first column. Next have them discuss with their talking partners what they think should be written in the other three columns.

"*Why* do you think Clover and Anne do this?"

"What do Clover and Anne *get* out of doing it?"

"What does this tell us about Clover and Anne and our *theme* of friendship?"

Complete the Thinking Theme Chart together. For this first lesson, you may want to model choosing the events to write in the first column so that your students begin to understand that the events chosen should show something about the theme.

Thinking Theme Chart for Friendship

Big Question:			
How do you think Clover and Anne show friendship?			
Event or **actions** by characters connected to the theme, including examples and nonexamples	**Why** does the character act this way?	What does the character **get** for acting this way?	Does this event show the **theme** of friendship? Yes, because *or* No, because
Anne asks to play jump rope with the girls and Sandra says no.	She wants to play with the girls. She is looking for friends.	She gets rejected by the girls and has no chance to play.	Yes, because Anne is trying to make a friend. No, because Clover and her friends reject the attempt.
Clover gets close to the fence, and Anne asks Clover her name.	The girls want to be friends. They want to spend time together. You have to talk to get to know each other. They are curious about each other.	They get a chance to talk.	Yes, friends start with exchanging names.

continued

The First Thinking Theme Lesson Using a Read-Aloud Text

Clover and Anne sit on the fence all summer, even when the other girls give them funny looks.	They are loyal to each other; they are nice to each other in front of other people; they decide to be friends no matter what other people think.	They get to spend time together; they form a new friendship.	Yes, friendship is being together in front of others and spending time talking.
Clover and Sandra jump rope while Anne twirls it.	There is room for more people in a friendship. You can be nice to lots of people.	They make more friends.	Yes, friends have fun playing.
All the girls sit on the fence, chatting.	They want to talk. They are now friends.	They get friendship and time to be together.	Yes, because once you get to know someone, you realize people are mostly the same.

Complete the Friendship Concept Chart by adding examples and nonexamples from the story.

Concept Chart for Friendship

Examples (from own life)

Played together nicely
Gave someone a pencil
Sat with the new kid at lunch
Asked someone their name

Nonexamples (from own life)

Stuck out tongue
Ignored someone
Not sharing stuff;
Saying "You cannot play!"

Definition:

Friendship —
is when friends
spend time
together, show
kindness to each
other, and are
loyal to each
other

Example characteristics

Getting along with people
Sharing with everyone
Taking turns at home and school

Nonexample characteristics

Fighting and disagreeing
Kicking, being mean, pushing
Calling names and being rude,
Ignoring others

Examples from books

Anne and Clover sit on the fence
  talking.
All the girls sit on the fence
  talking.
The girls jump rope together.

Nonexamples from books

Sandra tells Anne she can't jump.

Have the class work together in a shared writing format to construct an answer to the big question, backing up their opinions with facts and details from the story. Here is what the shared writing piece might look like:

> Clover and Anne show many examples of friendship in the book The Other Side. Friendship is spending time together, showing kindness to each other, and being loyal to someone. Anne and Clover spend time together sitting on the fence talking because they aren't allowed to go inside each other's house or in each other's yard. This gives them a chance to get to know each other better. They show kindness to each other by complimenting each other's houses and laundry. They smile at each other when they are shopping with their moms. Another way they show each other friendship is tough for kids. They are true and loyal in front of other people. When the other girls look at them funny, they sit on the fence anyway. They like each other and want to spend time playing and talking. Clover and Anne build a friendship on a fence by understanding what it takes to be friends.

Work Together to Use the Thinking Theme Checklist to Evaluate This Response

Thinking Theme Checklist for One Text
❏ 1. Do I take a position and clearly answer the question?
❏ 2. Do I include my definition of the theme?
❏ 3. Do I support my answer with specific examples and details from the selection?
❏ 4. Is my response complete?

When you have completed this first Thinking Theme lesson, you will have taught your students many concepts they will need to be successful when they do lessons in which they must take responsibility for both reading the text and theme thinking in that text. Important things your students should have learned include the following:

● *What a theme is.* A *theme* is a big idea that a story is all about. We pay attention to what characters do and think about why they do them in order to figure out what the author is trying to teach us about the theme. The theme Concept Chart summarizes what we know about theme from our experiences and what we learn from our reading.

- *What a big question is.* The *big question* is the question we answer when we have finished the story and the charts. To answer the big question, we have to think deeply about the theme and the characters.

- *How we think when we are thinking themes.* When we are thinking themes, our job is to pay attention to what characters do and think about why they do these things and what they get out of doing them. We also think about what the characters' actions show about the theme.

- *What to do when we get to a sticky flag.* When we get to a sticky flag, we *stop, think, and talk.* We try to see if there are any events we want to add to the Thinking Theme Chart and what we think should go in the other three columns.

- *How to answer the big question.* When we have finished the story and the charts, we answer the big question. We use facts and details from the story to back up our opinions.

- *How to evaluate our response.* We use the Thinking Theme Checklist to evaluate our responses.

Stop and think!

Use Shared Reading or Read-Along for Your Next Thinking Theme Lessons

Once your students are well on their way to understanding theme thinking during a teacher read-aloud, your next step might be to let them share the reading as they do the theme thinking. Choose a different theme from the one you focused on during your read-aloud lessons, but still choose one that is quite familiar to your children. If you chose friendship for your first lessons, next you might want to consider cooperation (which we call *working together* with our youngest children) or integrity (which we call *honesty.*) Here are some books commonly available in big-book format and the themes they work well for:

- *Farmer Duck,* by Martin Waddell (working together, cooperation)
- *The Little Red Hen,* by Lucinda McQueen (doing your part, responsibility)
- *Guess How Much I Love You,* by Nick Butterworth (caring)
- *The Doorbell Rang,* by Pat Hutchins (sharing)
- *The Carrot Seed,* by Ruth Krauss (perseverance)
- *Swimmy* (cooperation)

You can do a shared reading lesson even if the book you choose is not available in big-book format. Consider making transparencies of the pages and showing them on an overhead projector or having two or three children share a book so they can read along with you.

When we use shared reading as the way to read the text for a Thinking Theme lesson, we often read the whole book to our students for the first reading and then read the book again with the children chiming in as they are able. We usually read the book to them the first time without any attention to the theme—no Concept Chart, no big question, no Thinking Theme Chart. Just read it to students and enjoy the book. (Do, however, "picture walk" the book before this first reading, introducing important characters and key vocabulary.)

After this first reading, tell the children that you have noticed there is a big idea, a theme that the author wants readers to think about in this book. Share three scenarios you have created that you know your students will relate to, and let them talk about their experiences with the theme in small groups. Then create your Concept Chart.

Next show the children the Thinking Theme Chart, on which you have written the big question at the top. Have students read the big question with you, and tell them that the information they help you list in the columns will help them answer the big question.

Between the first and second reading, attach sticky flags to the places where you want your students to stop, think, and talk. Arrange your students so they are sitting close to their talking partners. Read the book again, and invite children to join in the reading as they are able to. Tell children that in addition to helping you read, their job is to think about the big question and what to add to the Thinking Theme Chart.

Stop and think!

Continue reading until you come to a sticky flag. Ask children to talk with their partners and see if they think anything has happened in the story that shows anything about the theme. Point to the columns on your Thinking Theme Chart, and remind students they are trying to think of actions the characters do that show something about the theme, why the characters do these things, what they get out of doing these things, and what they show us about the theme.

As the children talk, listen in on some of their conversations and redirect their attention to the Thinking Theme Chart questions if they lose their focus. After no more than two minutes, tell the children that partner talking time is over, and ask them to share what events they have noticed and their ideas about these events. Record their ideas on the chart.

Continue the shared reading until you come to the end of the page with the next sticky flag. The children should eagerly begin talking with their partners because by now they are anticipating a stop, think, and talk point and are beginning to understand what they are to talk about.

Continue reading until you have finished the book, stopping at each sticky flag. (Have no more than two or three for these early lessons.) Record the information in the columns as children share it. When they can't agree, record their dissenting ideas if they can back them up based on what they have read. Be sure to turn back and have them reread parts of the text if this will help them clarify their thinking. When no one can come up with a good answer to write in a column, just put some question marks in that box and move on. Deep thinking about characters and theme is your goal. The chart is there to help you and your students structure that thinking. Thinking and discussion—not completing a neat, tidy chart—are what a Thinking Theme lesson is all about. Balance the recording on the chart and the discussion; don't let the filling in the chart interrupt good conversation.

After you have completed the story and the chart, review what you have recorded on the Thinking Theme Chart. Then complete the Concept Chart by adding examples and nonexamples (if there are any—sometimes texts with strong themes contain nonexamples, and sometimes they don't!). Have the big question read aloud, and have children compose an answer to that question using details and facts from the texts. You may want the talking partners to orally compose an answer to the big question and then have them share their ideas with you as you record their thoughts to produce a shared writing response.

Depending on how well you think your children are learning the procedures for Thinking Theme lessons and whether another engaging book is available on the same theme, you may want to do a second lesson. If you do, go through the same procedures as the first lesson, beginning by reviewing the Concept Chart and returning to this chart to add examples and nonexamples from the second selection. Depending on the age and ability of your children, you may also want them to help you with the harder task of composing a response comparing the theme across the two selections.

Don't be afraid to keep your students with you in a read-aloud or shared reading format early in the year. It may feel like you are giving them too much support (particularly with older children), but the time invested in helping them learn how to think themes, how to talk with partners about themes, how to complete the Thinking Theme Chart, and how to compose a response to the big question will pay off later in the year when you ask them to take responsibility for reading and thinking. Remember your big goal: By the end of the year, you want all your students to be able to read a text on their own level independently, identify the theme, and write a response in which they talk about how the characters demonstrate the theme.

Teach Students to Think Themes as They Partner Read the Selection

Once your students have learned the Thinking Theme procedures, it is time to teach them how to read in partners. Partner reading is a very effective way to organize your students to read and think. Two heads are indeed better than one.

The key is to make sure students know how to read and think together. You have already begun to teach them to think with a partner by seating them in talking partners when you do a read-aloud or shared reading of a text. They know what they are to talk about—

information to add to the Thinking Theme Chart. They also know when to stop, think, and talk—when they get to a sticky flag you have placed strategically in the text. To make partner reading work in your classroom, consider these tips from teachers who use partner reading regularly and effectively.

Stop and think!

Arrange the Partnerships Thoughtfully

Who to partner with whom is the first and most important decision you will make. Children who do not like each other will not read and think well together. For your struggling readers, you need to find partners who can and will help them read and think—without making them feel bad about their ability. The best readers in your classroom are probably not the best partners for your struggling readers. Often, the best readers are impatient with others who cannot quickly do what seems so simple to them. The best partners for your struggling readers are usually average or slightly below-average readers who are also kind and agreeable people. Some teachers find that they can begin thinking about who to partner together by ranking their readers from best to worst and then making the initial pairings by pairing child 1 with a child halfway down the list and child 24 (assuming you have 24 children) with a child halfway up the list. If you begin with this method, your initial pairings might be as follow:

1 with 12	2 with 11	3 with 10
4 with 9	5 with 8	6 with 7
24 with 13	23 with 14	22 with 15
21 with 16	20 with 17	19 with 18

Once you have done this, look at the pairings and think about how willing the paired children will be to work together. If 5 and 8 don't get along, pair 5 with 7 and 8 with 6. Your goals are to have struggling readers partnered with average or slightly below-average readers and to have everyone partnered with someone they like (though probably not their best friend)! If you have an odd number of children, create one triad (group of three). It should probably consist of three of your average to above-average readers and three very agreeable children.

When you have decided on the pairings, try them out for a few lessons. Spend your coaching time with any partners who seem to have difficulty working together, and see if you can help them learn how to do so. After several partner reading days, adjust the partnerships as needed so that the partners are working together as well as they can, given the particular mix of children you have this year. When you are satisfied that you have created the best partnerships, use them whenever you do partner reading. Changing partners means your children will have to renegotiate their working relationships. The energy they will spend on this would be better spent reading and thinking.

Role-Play and Model How You Want Partners to Read Together

The first time you put children into partners to read together, make clear what you expect them to do. Choose a child to be your partner, and role-play partner reading. If you want children to take turns reading pages, tell them you are going to take turns and then do it. When reading, make sure you make a mistake and come to one word you need help figuring out. Alert your partner ahead of time that you will be doing this, and have him or her help you figure out the word or correct your mistake in a nice and helpful way. When you come to a sticky flag, model stopping, thinking, and talking about the character and theme, referring to the chart to focus your talking.

Stop and think!

After role-playing partner reading, discuss with students what they saw. Ask these questions about your role-play with partner Billy:

- How did we know who should read? (You took turns on some pages, and on some pages you read together.)
- What did Billy do when I read *comforted* instead of *comfortable?* (He told you the word and showed you the *-able* at the end and said that was a very good try for a big word.)
- What did Billy do when I couldn't figure out a word? (He helped you by telling you that the word ended in *–ace,* like *face.*)
- Did Billy make me feel stupid because I didn't read it perfectly? (No, he helped you very nicely!)
- What did we do when we got to a sticky flag? (You stopped and talked.)
- What did we talk about? (Those things on the chart—what the character did and why, what the character got, and what that told us about how honest he was.)

After this role-play and debrief, have your children read the selection (including the part you and Billy just read) with their partners. Tell them that as they read, you will be coming around and "spying" on them. Resist the temptation to coach today, as you will when students have mastered the partner reading routines. Rather, lurk near each partnership like a detective and write down the good partner behaviors you spy as they read. When reading time is up, gather your students together and tell them the good partner behaviors you spied. Name names and be specific. Children are always impressed when teachers pay such good attention to what they were doing. Here are some examples of specific comments:

"Abby and Jeni were doing some very good thinking. They got to the second flag and Jeni said, 'I know an event that meant she wasn't being honest.' Abby said, 'I agree and I know why she lied. She was afraid she wouldn't get to go to the sleepover if she told the truth.'"

"Brad was really helpful when Carlton couldn't figure out a word. He said, 'Look at the picture and think about how she feels. It's another word for scared.'"

Only comment on the positive things you see, and make your comments specific, using the exact words your students used as much as possible. All students want our attention, and soon they will all be doing their best to be "caught" being really helpful and doing good thinking.

Set a Time Limit and a Timer as Partners Read

It is essential that you tell your students how long they have to read the selection. Since you will be circulating and coaching partners as they read, you can't be the one who keeps the time. When you tell children they have fourteen minutes to read and think about the selection, you have to stick with that time limit, or soon they won't pay any attention to what you say about how much time they have. Most teachers who find partner reading effective set a timer to keep everyone on track. When the timer sounds, some partners may not be finished. Resist the temptation to wait for everyone to finish. You will not have enough time for the thinking and talking required to complete the Thinking Theme Chart, which is how children will learn to think deeply about characters and theme.

When the timer sounds and a few children say, "We're not done yet," you have two choices. Some teachers say,

> "That's fine. Join us anyway. You can help us talk about the events that happened early in the story and will learn how the story ends from listening to the ideas of your friends who did finish it."

Other teachers respond to "We're not finished" by saying,

> "That's fine. Keep reading until you do finish, and then join us at the chart."

Both these alternatives work well and allow you to get on with the important after-reading thinking. Pick the one you like and stick to it. You will be amazed at how children can pace themselves to finish when they know you will stick to the time limit and it doesn't ruffle you when they have not finished!

Include a Disincentive for Finishing Early

Another timing issue has to do with children who finish before the timer sounds. "We're done," they chime gleefully, and soon everyone is in "race mentality" and trying to finish. This racing through the reading does not encourage deep thinking. So whenever your children are reading in partners, tell them what to do if they finish before the time is up:

> "You have thirteen minutes to read and think today. Remember that you should stop and talk with your partner at every sticky flag. See how many events you can find that

say something about the theme and think about what you would put in *Why* and *Get* columns. If you finish all your reading and thinking and there are still a few minutes left, take out a piece of paper and write down the event you think tells the most about the theme, why you think the character does this, what the character gets out of it, and what it tells us about the theme. If you do this for one event and you still have time, choose a second event and do the same thing."

When children go to partner read, they should always know the purpose for reading, how long they have to do it, and what they are to do if they finish before the timer sounds. For a Thinking Theme lesson, what they should do is to write down information to add to the chart. Writing this down is not very appealing, however. Teachers who make it clear what partners are expected to do if they finish early and then hand a piece of paper to partners who have chimed "We're done" will tell you that somehow, magically, after a few partner reading sessions, no one ever finishes early! Most children like to talk about what happened and why. Most don't like to write it. If they do finish early, they learn to go back, reread, and talk, trying not to look like they're done so they won't have to write.

As Partners Read, Circulate and Coach Students on Reading and Thinking

Once partner routines have been established, you have a wonderful opportunity to coach and monitor your students' word identification and thinking. Stop in with as many partnerships as you can, and observe how they are helping each other both with the words and the thinking. Don't ignore the partnerships that include the children in the top half of your class, who are usually happy with just a minute of your time and a word or two of your praise for what good thinking they are doing. Spend more time with the partnerships that contain children in the bottom half of your class. These are the children who need more support and who will benefit most from your individual attention.

Use a Three-Ring Circus Format to Provide the Right Amount of Support

After your children are reading well with partners, you may decide on some days to have some of your students read with you and to have some of your better readers read and think by themselves. When some children are reading in a group with the teacher, some are reading with partners, and some are reading by themselves, we have a *three-ring circus*. Most teachers create a poster on which they put students' names in the appropriate circles so everyone will know how they will read the selection today. To make this easy and reusable, create three circles on a laminated board. Then you can easily erase the old names and add new names each time you decide to use this reading format.

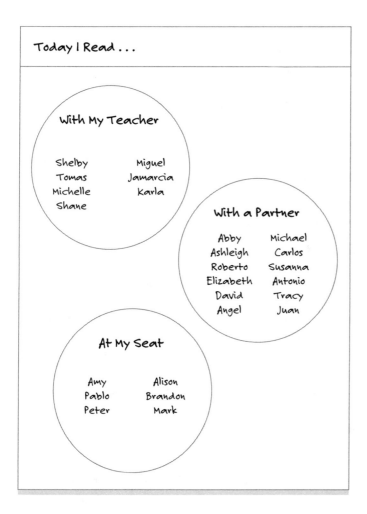

Today I Read . . .

With My Teacher

Shelby   Miguel
Tomas   Jamarcia
Michelle   Karla
Shane

With a Partner

Abby   Michael
Ashleigh   Carlos
Roberto   Susanna
Elizabeth   Antonio
David   Tracy
Angel   Juan

At My Seat

Amy   Alison
Pablo   Brandon
Peter   Mark

If you decide to organize your classroom into a three-ring circus, think carefully about whom you assign to each ring. Only the children you are quite certain can handle reading and thinking on their own should be assigned to work by themselves. Remember that they will not have anyone to talk to when they get to a sticky flag. These must be in-dependent and focused students.

Your natural tendency will probably lead you to keep your most struggling readers with you, but you need to be sure to include a good reading model or two. You want some good thinkers in your group, and you don't want your students to start thinking of the group you are working with as the low reading group. ("How can this possibly be the low group if Tracy is here?")

Use the three-ring circus format only after your children are automatic at following the partner routines and are very clear about their job in reading a Thinking Theme lesson.

Stop and think!

Make sure you let students know that the partner reading rules also apply to a three-ring circus. Set the timer and remind students what to do if they should finish early.

When you are reading with your coaching group during a three-ring circus, use this opportunity to help them focus on characters and theme. Stop everyone at each sticky flag and talk though all the events, whys, gets, and theme connections. Don't worry if your group doesn't finish the selection in the allotted time. They can hear how the story ends by the sharing that gets done as the Thinking Theme Chart gets filled in. You can choose to keep a small group of children with you to coach them on deep thinking. It's better to accomplish this goal well with a portion of the text than to rush through just so they read it all.

Stop and think!

Have Students Read the Selection in Teams or Play-School Groups

Did you ever play school when you were a child? Did you ever round up the neighborhood children and pretend you were the teacher? Did you ever play school with your dolls and stuffed animals as your students? Most elementary teachers played school when they were little, and most children enjoy playing school. For a change of pace in the latter part of the school year, form children into play-school groups with four or five students in each group. (Some older children will be insulted by the idea of working in play-school groups, so just do it the same way but call them *teams*. The teacher in each group can be called the *coach*.)

Most teachers find it works best to include in each group a good reader, a few average readers, and a struggling reader. Each group will read the selection you have chosen, stopping at the sticky flags and talking about what should go on the chart. Most teachers find it works best to have the children read the selection together in choral reading fashion when they are a play-school group. When they finish reading, they will fill in the chart together as a group.

Stop and think!

If you do play-school groups or teams, rotate the job of teacher or coach. This person's job is to keep everyone on track. Even a struggling reader can be the coach because the coach's jobs are to keep everyone focused, to make sure the chart questions get answered, and to make sure everyone's opinions are respected. For writing the answers on the chart, you may want to appoint a recorder in each group, or you may want different children assigned to different columns. If you have five students in the group, give the students who are not the teacher cards labeled **Event, Who, Get,** and **Theme** to indicate which column of the chart they are responsible for writing. The teacher in this case will not be writing but should be keeping everyone on task.

The real advantage of play-school groups or teams is that you have a lot more participation. Working in these small cooperative groups, all children can share a lot more of their thinking and more voices can be heard in the same amount of time. When the charts have been completed, gather the whole class together and compare the charts. There will be many events and information that the groups agree on, but there will also be differences. Remind students that when they are thinking theme, they are doing deep thinking about what events are important, why the characters do what they do, what they get out of doing this, and what this tells about the theme. Sometimes it is easy to determine these big ideas, but often it is hard to know for sure what characters are really thinking. Focus on the areas of agreement and use the points of disagreement to remind students that when they are thinking about the really big ideas, what matters is not that they all agree but that they can use the facts and details to justify their thoughts. Our experience with Thinking Theme lessons done in play-school groups or teams is that the groups always work hard to come up with good ideas and they are always eager to see what the other groups have come up with.

Use Book Club Groups to Make Thinking Theme Lessons More Multilevel

Another kind of cooperative group you can use to organize your Thinking Theme lessons is the book club group (Hall & Tillman, 2004). When children read in book club groups, they don't all read the same book. In fact, we plan for book club groups by choosing four books that are tied together in some way. The four books might all be by the same author, in the same genre, or on the same topic. For Thinking Theme lessons, we choose four books or stories with a common theme. For the theme of problem solving, for example, you might choose *Ruby the Copycat,* by Peggy Rathmann; *Legend of the Indian Paint-brush,* by Tomie de Paola; *Elmer,* by David McKee; and *Peter's Chair,* by Ezra Jack Keats. In all these books, the main character or characters have a problem and, like Buzzy the bumblebee, they have to try to solve it. When we choose books, we try to select one book that is harder than the others, one that is easier, and two at about the average reading level of the class. For this problem-solving Thinking Theme lesson, *Legend of the Indian Paint-brush* is clearly harder, and *Peter's Chair* is clearly easier.

We begin our Thinking Theme lesson by bringing out a Concept Chart we did previously on problem solving. We review what we learned about problem solving and from Buzzy the bumblebee.

We then show the children the four books we have chosen and explain that problem solving is an important theme in all of them. We explain that we don't have enough time or enough books for everyone to read all four books. So each student is going to make a first, second, and third choice of which book to read. We then show students four Thinking Theme Charts with these four big questions at the tops:

> **Big Question:** Ruby has one big problem and many small problems to solve. Do you think Ruby is a good problem solver?
>
> **Big Question:** Peter has one big problem to solve. Do you think Peter is a good problem solver?

Big Question: Little Gopher has one big problem and many small problems to solve. Do you think Little Gopher is a good problem solver?

Big Question: Elmer has one big problem to solve. Do you think Elmer is a good problem solver?

Next we explain the process to students:

"Today I am going to read the first section of each book to you. Your job, as always, is to listen for things the characters do that have something to do with solving a problem and then think about why the characters probably do that, what the characters get out of doing that, and whether this is a good example of problem solving. After each section I read, we will begin each Thinking Theme Chart by filling in the columns for one or two events from the first section of each book. In addition, you have another very important job today. When we get all four sections read and all four Thinking Theme Charts started, I am going to ask you to write down your first, second, and third choice for the book you want to read in your book club group."

Read aloud from each book until you reach the first sticky flag; then stop and let all the children think about an event that says something about the character and problem solving to list in column 1. Use the usual procedure of letting children talk with their talking partners about why the character does this action, what the character gets out of doing this, and what this action or event tells about the theme. Record students' ideas for one event on each chart.

Stop and think!

When you have read the first part of each book to everyone and have all the Thinking Theme Charts started with one event, ask your children to write down their three choices for which book they would like to read. Choice is an important motivator, and children of any age think more when they have a choice to make. As you collect the papers with students' choices, promise them that you will give each person one of his or her choices. But because you only have three copies of each book and because you don't want the groups to be too large, not everyone will get his or her first or even second choice.

Once you have the choices, forming the book club groups is quick and simple. Look first at the choices of your struggling readers. If the easier book (which, of course, you have not identified to anyone) is one of their choices, put them in the group with the easy book. Next look at the choices of your most advanced readers. If the harder book is one of their choices, put them in that group. Don't be surprised when one of your struggling students does not pick the easier book or one of your advanced students does not pick the harder book. Regardless, every child must be given one of his or her choices. Give struggling children who didn't choose the easier book their first choice, as long as it isn't the harder book. If they get their first choice, they will work harder. Give advanced readers who didn't choose the harder book one of their choices—but not the easier book.

. . . . •

111

Look at the choices of your average readers last. If one or two of your average readers listed the easier book as their first choice, add them to that group because they can help you assist struggling readers. If one or two of your average readers chose the harder book as their first choice, add them to that group, since the high readers will assist them. Distribute the remaining children so that you form four groups of five or six students, giving as many their first choices as possible. Write the names of the children in each group on the appropriate Thinking Theme Chart.

Thinking Theme Chart—Book Club 1

Big Question:

Ruby has one big problem and many small problems to solve. Do you think Ruby is a good problem solver?

Ruby the Copycat Book Club Members: David, Andrew, Ashleigh, Hannah, Maria, Carl

Event or **actions** by characters connected to the theme, including examples and nonexamples	**Why** does the character act this way?	What does the character **get** for acting this way?	Does this event show the **theme** of problem solving? Yes, because *or* No, because
Ruby returns to school wearing a bow in her hair that is just like Angela's.	She wants to fit in. She wants Angela to like her.	She gets a compliment from Angela.	Yes, because she feels part of the class.

Thinking Theme Chart—Book Club 2

Big Question:

Peter has one big problem to solve. Do you think Peter is a good problem solver?

Peter's Chair Book Club Members: Susie, Michael, Grant, Carolyn, Abby

Event or **actions** by characters connected to the theme, including examples and nonexamples	**Why** does the character act this way?	What does the character **get** for acting this way?	Does this event show the **theme** of problem solving? Yes, because *or* No, because
Peter looks at his mom fussing with the baby's cradle.	He is curious about what his mom is doing.	He gets a reminder that his crib is now painted pink.	No, he is not talking to his mom, so he won't solve his problem.

Thinking Theme Chart—Book Club 3

Big Question:			
Little Gopher has one big problem and many small problems to solve. Do you think Little Gopher is a good problem solver?			
Legend of the Indian Paintbrush Book Club Members: Andrew, Rebecca, Tommie, Daniel, Julie			
Event or **actions** by characters connected to the theme, including examples and nonexamples	**Why** does the character act this way?	What does the character **get** for acting this way?	Does this event show the **theme** of problem solving? Yes, because or No, because
Little Gopher goes to the hills alone to think about becoming a man.	He is still unhappy that he can't go on the hunt with the others.	He gets a vision from an Indian maiden and an old grandfather, who tell him that painting will make him famous among his people.	??

Thinking Theme Chart—Book Club 4

Big Question:			
Elmer has one big problem to solve. Do you think Elmer is a good problem solver?			
Elmer Book Club Members: Steven, Joseph, Mario, Elizabeth			
Event or **actions** by characters connected to the theme, including examples and nonexamples	**Why** does the character act this way?	What does the character **get** for acting this way?	Does this event show the **theme** of problem solving? Yes, because or No, because
Elmer goes into the woods.	He thinks others are laughing at him.	He gets time alone.	No, because running away doesn't solve problems.

When it is reading time the next day, gather the children and show them the charts. Announce proudly that it wasn't easy, but you were able to give all of them one of their choices! Review with everyone the problem-solving Concept Chart and the events written on each Thinking Theme Chart. Tell the children how many minutes they have to read the next portion of the text and where each book club group is to meet. Appoint a leader in each group, whose job it is to keep everyone on track. Hand the chart and a marker to one group member who can write well, and tell that person he or she is the recorder for the group.

Circulate and coach the groups, making sure they are focusing on the characters' actions and what they reveal about the theme. When the reading and charting time is up, gather the whole class together. Ask each group to hold up their chart and tell about events and what they thought about them. Since everyone heard the first part of each story yesterday, the children are usually very eager to hear more. Continue this procedure of letting the groups meet to read and chart as much text as you designate each day and ending the reading time by letting each group share what they learned.

Thinking Theme Chart—Book Club 1: Completed

Big Question:
Ruby has one big problem and many small problems to solve. Do you think Ruby is a good problem solver?

Ruby the Copycat Book Club Members: David, Andrew, Ashleigh, Hannah, Maria, Carl

Event or actions by characters connected to the theme, including examples and nonexamples	Why does the character act this way?	What does the character get for acting this way?	Does this event show the theme of problem solving? Yes, because or No, because
Ruby returns to school wearing a bow in her hair that is just like Angela's.	She wants to fit in. She wants Angela to like her.	She gets a compliment from Angela.	Yes, because she feels part of the class.
Ruby cries after Angela tells her that she hates her.	Her feelings are hurt.	She gets a talk from her teacher about copying other people and about being yourself.	No, because hurt feelings never solve anything.
Ruby peels off the fingernail.	She realizes she doesn't have to be like Angela or Miss Hart.	She gets to take off the fingernails, and she gets to realize that she doesn't need them.	Yes, she is starting to realize that she is her own person.
Ruby hops around in her room—forward, backward, sideways—with her eyes shut.	She wants to show that she can do something that no one else is doing.	Her class compliments her for being the best hopper ever.	Yes, because everyone realizes that Ruby is special, too.

Thinking Theme Chart—Book Club 2: Completed

Big Question:
Peter has one big problem to solve. Do you think Peter is a good problem solver?

Peter's Chair Book Club Members: Susie, Michael, Grant, Carolyn, Abby

Event or **actions** by characters connected to the theme, including examples and nonexamples	**Why** does the character act this way?	What does the character **get** for acting this way?	Does this event show the **theme** of problem solving? Yes, because or No, because
Peter looks at his mom fussing with the baby's cradle.	He is curious about what his mom is doing.	He gets a reminder that his crib is now painted pink.	No, he is not talking to his mom, so he won't solve his problem.
Peter picks up the chair and runs away with it.	He doesn't want his dad to paint it pink for the baby.	He gets the chair so that it can't be painted. He also gets a chance to calm down.	No, running away won't solve his problem.
Peter paints the little chair pink.	He is ready to share and accept his baby sister.	He gets time with his dad, love for his sister, and something fun to do.	Yes, because he is cooperating with his dad to solve his problem.

Thinking Theme Chart—Book Club 3: Completed

Big Question:
Little Gopher has one big problem and many small problems to solve. Do you think Little Gopher is a good problem solver?

Legend of the Indian Paintbrush Book Club Members: Andrew, Rebecca, Tommie, Daniel, Julie

Event or **actions** by characters connected to the theme, including examples and nonexamples	**Why** does the character act this way?	What does the character **get** for acting this way?	Does this event show the **theme** of problem solving? Yes, because or No, because
Little Gopher goes to the hills alone to think about becoming a man.	He is still unhappy that he can't go on the hunt with the others.	He gets a vision from an Indian maiden and an old grandfather, who tell him that painting will make him famous among his people.	??

Little Gopher begins to paint scenes of great hunts, great deeds, and great Dream-Visions.	He does this because he is told to do so in the great Dream-Vision on top of the hill.	He gets paintings that tell the stories of his people.	Yes, because he is trying to figure out what the visions mean.
Little Gopher returns to the hillside to paint the perfect sunset.	He wants his paintings to be very real and capture the beauty of his land.	He gets the perfect picture of a sunset and the admiration of his people, who now call him He-Who-Brought-the-Sunset-to-the-Earth.	Yes, he earns his name and the respect of the people.

Thinking Theme Chart—Book Club 4: Completed

Big Question:
Elmer has one big problem to solve. Do you think Elmer is a good problem solver?

Elmer Book Club Members: Steven, Joseph, Mario, Elizabeth

Event or **actions** by characters connected to the theme, including examples and nonexamples	**Why** does the character act this way?	What does the character **get** for acting this way?	Does this event show the **theme** of problem solving? Yes, because or No, because
Elmer goes into the woods.	He thinks others are laughing at him.	He gets time alone.	No, because running away doesn't solve problems.
Elmer rolls in elephant-colored berries.	He wants to look like the other elephants.	He gets to look like the others.	Yes, he blends in. No, he doesn't really want to look like the others.
Elmer yells and scares the elephants.	This is his personality. He wants attention.	He gets attention and laughter.	Yes, Elmer realizes the others like his personality.
Elmer is gray in parade when everyone else is weird colors.	He has confidence to be different.	He gets friends and attention. He remembers the day of big joke.	Yes, Elmer keeps his confidence and friends.

Use Book Club Groups to Make Thinking Theme Lessons More Multilevel

When all books have been read, charted, and shared, add examples and nonexamples of problem solving from all four books to your Concept Chart for Problem Solving. You may want to limit each group to one example or nonexample from their book to accomplish this in a reasonable time. Have the children individually write their responses to the big question, reminding them to back up their opinions with specific facts and details from their book. Have them self-evaluate their responses before turning them in.

Using book club groups is a motivating way to organize Thinking Theme lessons. Children are always more motivated to read when they are reading a book that they have chosen. Also, the fact that both struggling readers and advanced readers are reading material close to their level will let them succeed and grow in ability and confidence. Teachers and students who use book club groups as one of the major ways to organize reading instruction late in the year get a much needed burst of enthusiasm to see them though until summer.

The following table identifies other sets of books that will make good Thinking Theme book club lessons. If you look at these books, you can probably easily determine which one in each set is easier and which one is harder. Remember that once children are past the beginning reading stage, prior knowledge is the biggest determinant of how hard or easy a book is for them. Rely more on your own perception of your students' knowledge and interests than on published reading-level numbers when deciding if a book is harder or easier.

Books for Thinking Theme Book Club Lessons

Friendship	Acceptance	Courage	Integrity	Determination Perseverance
Swimmy, by Leo Lionni	*The Memory String,* by Eve Bunting	*A Picture Book of Martin Luther King,* by David Adler	*The Empty Pot,* by Demi	*Katy Did It,* by Victoria Boutis
Big Al and Shrimpy, by Andrew Clements	*The Rag Coat,* by Lauren Mills	*A Picture Book of Rosa Parks,* by David Adler	*The Paper Bag Princess,* by Robert Munsch	*My Sister Anne's Hands,* by Mary Beth Lorlecki
Pink and Say, by Patricia Polacco	*Train to Somewhere,* by Eve Bunting	*A Picture Book of Frederick Douglass,* by David Adler	*Molly Bannaky,* by Alice McGill	*Uncle Jed's Barbershop,* by Margaree King Mitchell
The Other Side, by Kathleen Woodson				

Do Some Thinking Theme Lessons in Which Groups Determine the Theme

In order for children to think about themes when they are reading on their own, you need to help them learn to determine the theme. To do so, choose a story that can be read in one day and that has a strong theme. Pull out three or four of completed theme Concept Charts, and review with students the kid-friendly definitions you constructed and the characteristics/noncharacteristics and examples/nonexamples you recorded on these charts. Put students into play-school groups or teams, and appoint a teacher/coach in each one. Tell the students that their first job is to read the story together and decide as a group what the theme is.

Circulate as the children read, and remind them that their only job today is to decide what the theme is. Help them to use the Concept Charts you reviewed to make their decision. When the time is up, ask each group to share the theme they identified. If you have chosen a story with a strong theme, the groups should be in agreement. If there is disagreement, ask the groups to justify their choices. If the group that chose a different theme from the one you had in mind can justify their choice, congratulate them on their good thinking and admit that the story has two strong themes!

On the following day, display the Thinking Theme Chart with a big question you construct based on the identified theme. Have students reread the selection in a different format (perhaps partners or a three-ring circus), and prepare for a Thinking Theme discussion that will lead to completion of the Thinking Theme Chart. After students have read the selection, continue with the usual steps of a Thinking Theme lesson. Record their thinking on the chart. Add examples and nonexamples of the theme to the appropriate Concept Chart. Have students write, share, and evaluate responses to a writing prompt you construct related to the big question.

After this initial lesson in which students determine the theme, you may want to follow the same procedures but have students read two stories with the same theme and identify the theme. You may also want to form book club groups in which the groups read books with different themes, determine the themes, and then complete the Thinking Theme Charts as groups.

When you get to the point where you expect students to determine theme, avoid introducing any new themes. Instead of having students spend time building the concept of a new theme, have them focus on how the now-familiar themes are demonstrated in a variety of stories.

By Year's End, Have Students Theme Thinking Independently

By the end of the year, your students should be able to read two selections on their level and write a response in which they compare the selections, linking characters and theme. Your students will be reading and writing on different levels, but they should all have learned how to think about characters and theme. By dividing this big goal into smaller tasks across the year—giving children whatever support they need to read and think about text and gradually giving them more responsibility—you will help your students achieve this goal.

References

Bloom, B. S. (1956). *Taxonomy of educational objectives.* New York: Longman.

Cunningham, P. M. (2006). High-poverty schools that beat the odds. *The Reading Teacher, 60,* 382–385.

Cunningham, P. M., Hall, D. P., & Sigmon, C. M. (1999). *The teachers' guide to the Four Blocks.* Greensboro, NC: Carson-Dellosa.

Durkin, D. (1978). What classroom observations reveal about reading comprehension instruction. *Reading Research Quarterly, 14,* 481–533.

Frayer, D., Frederick, W. C., & Klausmeier, H. J. (1969). *A schema for testing the level of cognitive mastery.* Madison: Wisconsin Center for Education Research.

Hall, D. P., & Tillman, C. (2004). *Book club groups.* Greensboro, NC: Carson-Dellosa.

Knapp, M. (1995). *Teaching for meaning in high-poverty classrooms.* New York: Teachers College Press.

Michigan Educational Assessment Program. (2005a, Fall). *Released items for English language arts—Grade 3: Scoring guide for released item #22.* Retrieved September 19, 2006, from www .michigan.gov/mde/0,1607,7-140-22709_31168_3135595471--,00.html

Michigan Educational Assessment Program. (2005b, Fall). *Released items for English language arts—Grade 4: Scoring guide for released item #22.* Retrieved September 19, 2006, from www .michigan.gov/mde/0,1607,7-140-22709_31168_3135595471--,00.html

Michigan Educational Assessment Program. (2005c, Fall). *Released items for English language arts—Grade 5: Scoring guide for released item #22.* Retrieved September 19, 2006, from www .michigan.gov/mde/0,1607,7-140-22709_31168_3135595471--,00.html

National Center for Education Statistics. (2004). Percentage of students, by reading achievement level, grade 4: 1992–2003. *The nation's report card: Reading.* Washington, DC: National Center for Education Sciences, U.S. Department of Education. Retrieved September 12, 2006, from http://nces.ed.gov/nationsreportcard/reading/results/2003/natachieve-g4.asp

Taylor, B. M., Pearson, P. D., Clark, K., & Walpole, S. (2000). Effective schools and accomplished teachers: Lessons about primary reading instruction in low-income schools. *Elementary School Journal, 10*(2), 121–166.

Common Themes and Books That Support Them

Problem Solving

Buzzy the Bumblebee, by Denise Brennan-Nelson (Sleeping Bear Press, 1999)

Peter's Chair, by Ezra Jack Keats (Puffin, 1998)

Elmer, by David McKee (HarperCollins, 1989)

Days with Frog and Toad, by Arnold Lobel (HarperTrophy, 1984)

Legend of the Indian Paintbrush, by Tomie de Paola (Putnam Juvenile, 1996)

Ruby the Copycat, by Peggy Rathmann (Scholastic Paperbacks, 2006)

Big Bushy Mustache, by Gary Soto (Knopf Books for Young Readers, 1998)

Friendship

The Other Side, by Jacqueline Woodson (Putnam, 2001)

Pink and Say, by Patricia Polacco (Philomel, 1995)

Big Al and Shrimpy, by Andrew Clements (Aladdin, 2005)

Swimmy, by Leo Lionni (Dragonfly Books, 1992)

A Week-End with Wendell, by Kevin Henkes (HarperTrophy, 1995)

Charlotte's Web, by E. B. White (HarperTrophy, 2006)

Franklin's New Friend, by Paulette Bourgeois (Scholastic, 1997)

Kindness/Sharing/Caring

Guess How Much I Love You, by Sam Mcbratney (Walker Books, 2006)

The Doorbell Rang, by Pat Hutchins (HarperTrophy, 1989)

Be Good to Eddie Lee, by Virginia Fleming (Putnam Juvenile, 1997)

Wilfred Gordan McDonald Partridge, by Mem Fox (Kane/Miller, 1989)

Betty Doll, by Patricia Polacco (Philomel Books, 2004)

Helping

The Wolf's Chicken Stew, by Keiko Kasza (Putnam Juvenile, 1987)

Franklin Helps Out, by Paulette Bourgeois (Scholastic Paperbacks, 2000)

The Teddy Bear, by David McPhail (Henry Holt, 2005)

Chicken Little, by Steven Kellogg (HarperTrophy, 1987)

Herman the Helper, by Robert Kraus (Aladdin, 1987)

Freedom

Old Henry, by Joan W. Blos (HarperTrophy, 1990)

The Big Orange Splot, by Daniel Manus Pinkwater (Scholastic Paperbacks, 1993)

Follow the Drinking Gourd, by Jeanette Winter (Dragonfly Books, 1992)

A Picture Book of Rosa Parks, by David A. Adler (Holiday House, 1993)

Determination/Perseverance

Uncle Jed's Barbershop, by Margaree King Mitchell (Aladdin Picture Books, 1998)

Brave Irene, by William Steig (Sunburst Books, 1988)

The Carrot Seed, by Ruth Krauss (HarperTrophy, 1993)

Sister Anne's Hands, by Marybeth Lorbiecki (Puffin, 2000)

Pink and Say, by Patricia Polacco (softcover) (Scholastic, 1995)

Katy Did It, by Victoria Boutis (William Morrow, 1982)

Jumanji, by Chris Van Allsburg (Scholastic, 1981)

Picnic at Mudsock Meadow, by Patricia Polacco (Putnam, 1992)

Baseball Saved Us, by Ken Mochizuki (Lee & Lowe Books, 1995)

Sarah, Plain and Tall, by Patricia MacLachlan (HarperTrophy, 2004)

The Little Engine That Could, by Watty Piper (Philomel, 2005)

Courage

Teammates, by Peter Golenbock (Voyager Books, 1992)

The Butterfly, by Patricia Polacco (Scholastic, 2001)

Sylvester and the Magic Pebble, by William Steig (Aladdin, 2006)

Ruby Mae Has Something to Say, by David Small (Knopf Books for Young Readers, 1992)

John Henry, by Julius Lester (Puffin, 1999)

The Sign of the Beaver, by Elizabeth George Speare (Yearling Books, 1994)

Thundercake, by Patricia Polacco (Putnam, 1997)

The Lily Cupboard: A Story of the Holocaust, by Shulamith Levey Oppenheim (HarperTrophy, 1995)

A Picture Book of Martin Luther King, by David A. Adler (Holiday House, 1989)

A Picture Book of Rosa Parks, by David A. Adler (Holiday House, 1993)

A Picture Book of Harriet Tubman, by David A. Adler (Holiday House, 1992)

A Picture Book of Frederick Douglass, by David A. Adler (Holiday House, 1993)

Working Together/Cooperation

The Great Big Enormous Turnip, by Alexi Tolstoy (Award Publications, 2003)

The Biggest Pumpkin Ever, by Steven Knoll (Cartwheel Books, 1993)

The Wednesday Surprise, by Eve Bunting (Clarion Books, 1989)

Stone Soup, by Marcia Brown (Aladdin, 2005)

Just a Little Bit, by Ann Tompert (Houghton Mifflin/Walter Lorraine Books, 1996)

Hannah, by Gloria Whelan (Random House, 1991)

Farmer Duck, by Martin Waddell (Walker Books, 2002)

Swimmy, by Leo Lionni (Dragonfly Books, 1973)

City Green, by DyAnne Disalvo-Ryan (HarperCollins, 1994)

Uncle Wille and the Soup Kitchen, by DyAnne Disalvo-Ryan (HarperTrophy, 1997)

Integrity/Honesty

Too Many Tamales, by Gary Soto (Putnam, 1996)

The Empty Pot, by Demi (Henry Holt, 1996)

The Paper Bag Princess, by Robert Munsch (Annick Press, 1992)

Molly Bannaky, by Alice McGill (Houghton Mifflin, 1999)

The Velveteen Rabbit, by Margery Williams (Atheneum/Anne Schwartz Books, 1999)

Believing Sophie, by Hazel Hutchins (Albert Whitman, 1995)

A Day's Work, by Eve Bunting (Clarion, 1997)

Harriet and the Garden, by Nancy Carlson (Carolrhoda Books, 2004)

Annabelle's Un-Birthday, by Steven Kroll (Atheneum, 1991)

Acceptance

The Rag Coat, by Lauren A. Mills (Little, Brown, 1991)

The Memory String, by Eve Bunting (Clarion, 2000)

Train to Somewhere, by Eve Bunting (Clarion Books, 2000)

Stand Tall, Molly Lou Melon, by Patty Lovell (Scholastic, 2001)

The Other Side, by Jacqueline Woodson (Putnam Juvenile, 2001)

Appelemando's Dreams, by Patricia Polacco (Putnam Juvenile, 1997)

My Rotten Red Headed Older Brother, by Patricia Polacco (Aladdin, 1998)

Mr. Lincoln's Way, by Patricia Polacco (Philomel, 2001)

Study Guide

This study guide is meant to assist your understanding of *Beyond Retelling: Toward Higher-Level Thinking and Big Ideas,* written by Patricia M. Cunningham and Debra Renner Smith. In the book, Cunningham and Smith show how teachers can guide students to participate in higher-level thinking by thinking deeply about the relationship between characters and theme.

The questions that follow are designed to enhance your understanding of the book and to help you make connections between the book and your work situation. You may use the study guide before or after you have read the book or as you finish each chapter. The study questions provided are not meant to cover all aspects of the book but rather to address specific ideas that might warrant further reflection.

The questions in this study guide are ones that you could generate on your own. They are typical questions that come to mind as readers read. Consider finding one reading partner and discussing these questions, using these questions in a grade-level discussion group, or using this study guide in a study group setting. There are many effective ways to use this study guide.

Chapter One: Why Higher-Level Thinking?

1. When the authors wrote, "Higher-level thinking is something that is much talked about but very seldom done," what was your reaction? Were you intrigued? Curious? What experiences did you have in your schooling with higher-level thinking instruction? Discuss how your schooling is different than the schooling your students are experiencing. Think about why higher-level thinking is taught in your situation.

2. According to the authors, higher-level thinking should be taught for several reasons: namely, it is the kind of thinking we do when we read, student engagement and motivation are increased when their opinions are valued, critical thinking is a recognized goal of the literacy curriculum, higher-level questions are one factor in increasing reading achievement, and end-of grade tests often include measures of higher-level thinking. Which of these reasons is most compelling to you? For what other reasons should we all try to increase the amount of higher-level thinking that occurs in our classrooms?

3. The authors wrote, "If the questions we pose don't have right or wrong answers, then how will we know if our students are comprehending? If their response to these questions is all discussion, then how will we evaluate the growth of individual students? Teachers who see the need for more higher-level thinking and try to promote it in their classrooms often become discouraged and defeated as they face the realities of accountability and evaluation." If you are teaching higher-level thinking, how do you grade it? Do you use rubrics? Do you use individual observation? How have you solved the evaluating question in your situation?

4. The authors conclude that all students can engage in deep thinking and benefit from Thinking Theme lessons. Do you agree or disagree? Do you think some students might need these lessons more than others or benefit more from them?

Chapter Two: The Big Question, the Big Idea, and Deep Thinking

1. What is the *big question?* How does the big question engage students in deep thinking?

2. What is *theme?* How is teaching about a theme of courage different than teaching about a topic such as *dinosaurs?* Why would students benefit from thinking about big ideas and lessons learned?

3. What is *Thinking Theme?* What type of books lend themselves best to these lessons? Where would Thinking Theme lessons fit into your curriculum?

4. Think of a book you have in your classroom or a story in your reading series that has a strong theme. To come up with the big question, look at the selection you are going to have your students read and think about the theme. Now write a big question for that book or story. Share your big question with your discussion group or reading partner.

Chapter Three: A Sample Thinking Theme Lesson

1. Chapter Three provides numerous examples of engaging students in learning. How does this teacher make sure that her students are all actively engaged in learning?

2. Instead of the teacher providing a *definition of the theme,* the students help to generate a kid-friendly definition. The teacher is prepared with a definition to assist in the conversation, if the students are stuck. Why is this an effective practice? How will you apply this to your situation?

3. The teacher uses a *Concept Chart* to help build understanding of the theme. How does generating examples of characteristics and nonexamples of characteristics deepen understanding?

4. The teacher offers three *scenarios* for discussion to enhance understanding of the concept of theme. Why three? Why not ten? Why not only one? When planning lessons for your classroom, brainstorming the scenarios ahead of time will help move the lesson along in your classroom. What did you notice about the discussion between the students? How did discussion help you as a reader?

5. The teacher poses a *big question,* which is written on the top of the Thinking Theme Chart. What key questions are also posed on the Thinking Theme Chart? How do these key questions help students understand the event?

6. After completing the Thinking Theme Chart, the teacher revisits the Concept Chart. How does adding *examples* and *nonexamples* from books help students understand the theme?

7. Effective direct instruction on how to think about theme is the premise of this book. In the context of this book, why does that make sense?

Chapter Four: Making the Concept of Theme Kid Friendly

1. The authors wrote at the beginning of Chapter Four, "In order to think deeply about a theme, children need to have a rich concept of what that theme means. Children cannot really consider how courageous a character is or which character shows the most integrity if they have a limited definitional knowledge of the key concept. It is not enough to know that *courage* is another word for *bravery* or that *integrity* means 'telling the truth.' Children need to have a rich knowledge of what these concepts mean if they are going to think deeply about them." How do you and your colleagues respond to this statement? Creating the theme Concept Chart is one way to develop the theme concept. In what other ways do you and your colleagues teach theme?

2. What is the *Frayer model?* Have you ever used Frayer model in your classroom? Can you envision the Frayer model being useful to you in other parts of your curriculum?

3. How do the scenarios assist students in understanding theme? What procedures does the teacher have in place to promote student engagement? How do you know that all students are learning? How do conversations between students in small groups assist all types of learners?

4. What did you notice about the pacing of the lesson? What techniques did the teacher use to assist in the pacing? What techniques do you use to move lessons along at a fast pace while still allowing students to learn?

Chapter Five: Linking Characters to Theme

1. The authors write, "Analyzing what characters do and say and how they interact is the key to helping students think about the theme." Relate that to the real characters that populate the stories of your real life. When you think of friends and relatives and themes such as integrity, courage, and loyalty, what actions come to mind? Without mentioning names, share some stories about real people and how their actions led you to make decisions about their character. Does this make real to you the link between characters' actions and theme?

2. The Thinking Theme Chart has four columns. After listing events or actions that tell us something about the theme, we think about why the character behaved in this way and what the character gets out of doing so. How would this kind of intentional thinking help your students do character analysis? Which of your students would profit most from this kind of systematic instruction in higher-level thinking?

3. When doing Thinking Theme lessons, we seat our students in talking partners. Before asking children to share their responses to the questions on the Thinking Theme Chart, we give them a brief time to talk with their partners about their answers. Why is this interaction important? How might this talking partner time be especially important for shy children or English language learners?

Chapter Six: Teaching Children to Write Responses about Characters and Themes

1. How does the teacher support writing a personal choice response? What students in your situation would benefit from this explicit instruction? What personal choice question will you ask your students?

2. The teacher demonstrates writing a personal choice response on a real-life topic of interest so that students learn the process. Why is personal choice important? How does personal choice help bridge the gap when learning a new concept? How do you find the balance between personal choice and applying learning to a process in your classroom?

3. The teacher demonstrates constructing a theme response based on one story. By explicitly guiding students through the first lesson, the teacher supports long-term learning. How did the teacher ensure that all the students would be successful in learning to write a written response?

4. The teacher demonstrates constructing a theme response based on two stories. A vital part of writing about the two stories is how they are alike and connected. How is writing about two stories different than writing about one?

5. How does using a checklist to evaluate writing help students? Have you ever used checklists or rubrics in your situation? How did your students respond to them?

Chapter Seven: A Sample Lesson Comparing Theme across Two Selections

1. What advantages do you see in helping students compare theme across two selections? Do you have other strategies for helping students make text-to-text connections? How does using two selections help students develop a deeper concept of the theme?

2. When using two selections, your big question needs to help students compare and contrast both selections. How much experience would your class need thinking about big questions for a single selection before they could successfully answer the big question comparing both selections?

3. The writing task for comparing two selections is more complicated. What could you do to give your students extra support when they begin writing responses comparing two selections?

Chapter Eight: Organizing for Thinking Theme Lessons across the Year

1. One type of gradual release is from full support in a lesson leading to total independence across several lessons. The goal is for all students to work by themselves at the end of the year. How does the teacher move students from the whole group, with everyone working together, to partnerships to small groups to independent workers? Is this a realistic goal? What does this look like in your situation?

2. The other type of gradual release is apparent within the lesson. The teacher provides more support for students at the beginning of each lesson and less at the end of the lesson. Which students will benefit most from this within-lesson gradual release of responsibility?

3. The chapter provides six different ways to organize your classroom for Thinking Theme lessons: read-aloud; shared reading/read-along; partner reading; play-school groups/teams; three-ring circus; book club groups. Which of these organizational structures do you currently use in your classroom? How are struggling students supported in each of these structures? What advantages do you see to including a variety of organizational structures as you teach Thinking Theme lessons?

Skeleton Charts and Checklists

Theme Concept Chart

Examples (from own life)	Nonexamples (from own life)
Example characteristics	**Nonexample characteristics**
Examples from books	**Nonexamples from books**

Definition:

Thinking Theme Chart

Big Question:			
Event or **actions** by characters connected to the theme, including examples and nonexamples	**Why** does the character act this way?	What does the character **get** for acting this way?	Does this event show the **theme** of _____? Yes, because *or* No, because

Thinking Theme Checklist for One Text

❑ 1. Do I take a position and clearly answer the question?

❑ 2. Do I include my definition of the theme?

❑ 3. Do I support my answer with specific examples and details from the selection?

❑ 4. Is my response complete?

Thinking Theme Checklist for Comparing Two Texts

❑ 1. Do I take a position and clearly answer the question?

❑ 2. Do I support my answer with specific examples and details from both selections?

❑ 3. Do I show how the two reading selections are alike or connected?

❑ 4. Is my response complete?

Index